ANDREW MARTIN is a prolific author of fiction and non-fiction books. His non-fiction has sometimes had a railway theme, and his novels include the award-winning 'Jim Stringer' thrillers, set on Britain's railways in the early 20th century, which have collectively sold over 300,000 copies. His most recent novels are *The Winker* (as AJ Martin) and *The Night in Venice*. His most recent non-fiction book is *Yorkshire: There and Back*. He writes the 'Reading on Trains' Substack, and his website is at martinesque.co.uk.

Praise for *Metropolitain*

'An eclectic blend of engineering and travelogue, urban planning and anecdote ... a sincere love letter'
The Economist

'Andrew Martin's entertaining study of the Parisian underground is a welter of timetables, carriage types, ticket colours and technical savvy'
Telegraph

'Delightful and diverting ... Martin is the most unpretentious and companionable of guides; the book is great fun'
Literary Review

'An utterly enjoyable voyage under Paris'
The Oldie

METROPOLITAIN

AN ODE TO THE PARIS METRO

ANDREW MARTIN

corsair

CORSAIR

First published in the United Kingdom in 2023 by Corsair
This paperback edition published in 2024

3 5 7 9 10 8 6 4

A CIP catalogue record for this book
is available from the British Library.

ISBN: 978-1-4721-5790-4

Printed and bound in Great Britain by
Clays Ltd, Elcograf S.p.A.

Papers used by Corsair are from well-managed forests
and other responsible sources.

MIX
Paper | Supporting
responsible forestry
FSC® C104740

Corsair
An imprint of
Little, Brown Book Group
Carmelite House
50 Victoria Embankment
London EC4Y 0DZ

An Hachette UK Company
www.hachette.co.uk

www.littlebrown.co.uk

'Suppose the way your transport system looked was just as important as the way it functioned.'

Daniel Wright
thebeautyoftransport.com

Contents

Dear Voyagers

For a long time, I was just *in the Metro*. I didn't know where I was in relation to the streets above, or even in relation to other lines. I started using the Metro in the 1970s, and it wasn't until the 1990s that the line colours – that crucial aide memoire on the map – settled down, having long been subject to some change and variation. I was in a kind of pleasant, fluid dream world, seemingly always amid white stations, with trains arriving quickly, before I could start to wonder where they might be going. The siren before the doors closed – like a sax tuning up – and the five notes on Spanish guitar preceding the incomprehensible announcements were like the soundtrack to a film in which I was merely an extra, but I was glad to be playing even such a minor role.

The more I used the Metro, the more I liked it, and admiration deepened to what I might almost call love, although I tend to think that word should be confined to human relations; therefore I ought not to say that I love Paris, but I do consider it the most beautiful city I have seen, and it was delightful to come to the slow realisation (even though it was perfectly logical) that its beauty was being perpetuated underground. At the risk of prolonging a perhaps mawkish theme, I can say that I love my wife, and since she was living in Paris when I got to know her (we'd first met in London), our courtship in the mid-1990s coincided with my most intense phase of Metro use, and this was a harmonious conjunction.

My very first feeling about the Metro was that it was efficient: I seldom had to wait more than a couple of minutes for a train, and I think I'd been riding the Metro for years before I found myself on a train that was stopped in a tunnel, but what came to entrance me was its visual style. It was elegant, in the sense of spare and economical. Indeed, I had first fretted that there wasn't enough *to* it. Most of the stations were simply white vaults, minimally embellished with signs in *blue* and white, as though further decorative embellishments were pending. The vaults generously straddled two tracks, rather than the fiddly practice of having one track per tunnel, as on the Tube lines properly so-called of the London Underground, so there was a relaxed openness to the Metro, which, unlike the London Underground, has never triggered my incipient claustrophobia. Most station entrances were also minimal: green railings around a tempting staircase (admittedly with dream-like iron replicas of plants, with lamps for flowers, sprouting from them in some cases). The trains were sparse, too – especially the older ones: white metal boxes on wheels, with hard seats. This sort of minimalism seemed part of the appeal of Paris in general, symbolising the confidence of the city. For a thing to work, it needn't be complicated; less is more.

In this sense, the Metro reminded me of a bar that used to be in the 6th Arrondissement until the elderly proprietress died or (as I prefer to think) retired to the South of France. The place reminded me of a 1950s kitchen: bright light, pale blue lino floor, Formica-topped tables of a similar colour and pine chairs. On the wall behind the counter was a menu featuring half a dozen drinks, corresponding to half a dozen bottles on the counter. As in one of Georges Simenon's Maigret novels, the default drink was white wine, which the proprietress measured out by filling small tumblers to the brim. All customers received a complimentary saucer-full of salted peanuts with each drink they ordered. The only other food option was a hard-boiled egg. A rack of these on the counter was topped off by a red plastic bauble, the one touch of bold colour in the place. There was no attempt to make the bar cosy, but it was a relaxing place to be nonetheless, everything being so simple and comprehensible, and it was always a bit of a wrench to leave.

I began to find the same about the Metro. If I took a train with the ostensible aim of going to some minor museum or gallery, I might (on arrival at the right station) weigh the prospect of my visit against the option of taking *another* train and deepening my acquaintance with the system – a chance to ponder, for example, its distinctive but elusive smell to which I was apparently becoming addicted. There have been many attempts to characterise this, as we will be seeing, but with its cloying but not unpleasant sweetness it reminded me of the emanations of the Rowntree's chocolate factory in my native city of York. (In 'Walk Like the Man', a piece about Hemingway's Paris for the *'Time Out' Book of Paris Walks*, Michael Palin wrote that the Metro 'smells of caramel'.) I also became fascinated by the various techniques of illuminating the white vaults. There is an almost cinematographic concern with lighting on the Metro.

I began to develop a list of places to go on the Metro, rather than places in Paris per se. I liked to make for those stretches where the train begins to tilt upwards, straining slightly to ascend – and then the City of Light is suddenly manifest in the most literal way with perhaps, the Eiffel Tower directly adjacent (if you're on Line 6), or Gare du Nord main-line station arrayed below (if you're on Line 2). Running along viaducts flamboyantly decorated with classical motifs, the elevated Metro seems high-spirited at having made an illicit escape. These trains, when not running directly alongside against tree-tops, give views directly into people's third-floor apartments: prosperous ones from Line 6, less prosperous ones from Line 2; and a photograph of any Metro train traversing the Seine would make a perfectly good postcard. I also liked visiting the ends of the lines, to run around the loops frequently sited at termini, which afford behind-the-scenes glimpses of lonely, troglodytic men tending parked trains, special signals, shadows and shafts of light intermingling.

On a day trip to Paris, I might spend more than half the time on the Metro. In fact, I once wrote an article about how to have a day out on the network, which I thought an original idea until I bought a book dating from 1970 called *On Rails Under Paris* by the curiously named B. J. Prigmore (who, incidentally, once wrote a book about Swiss railways with a C. W. Sex). Prigmore supplies an itinerary for just such a day, and we will be visiting most of the spots he recommended.

I began to read about the Metro as keenly as I'd once read about the London Underground, and this small book is intended to provide a shortcut to the things I most liked about the system. (It is small enough to be carried in a fairly large pocket, and I hope it will be so carried by readers touring the Metro, with the best possible companion a Metro map. For a free one, go to ratp.fr, click on 'Plans' at the top and, when the Metro map appears, click on 'Consulter le plan' to download the PDF, which prints nicely.)

I don't think the London Underground ever seduced me in the way the Metro did, but I found it fascinating on first acquaintance, and in both cases I had the useful perspective of the outsider: I'm an Englishman in Paris, just as I was a Yorkshireman in London. As a young man newly arrived in London I found the Underground exotic, eccentric, often beautiful. I was poised somewhere between nightmare and dream in a great tangle of tunnels that surely ought to be untangled according to some rational plan, but obviously that would be too expensive. And not only was I in it, but so was everyone else as well. I wanted to explain this bizarre phenomenon to myself, and to other people, so, after having written a newspaper column about the Underground for five years, I wrote a history of it, and lest I seem hard on the Underground in what follows, I would not have written that book had I not had a strong affection for it. In *Metropolitain*, I regularly invoke the London Underground for perspective, as a benchmark or comparison, which I think is valid because the London Underground was the world's *first* metro, and Paris, having taken a long cool look at it, decided to do the opposite. In some ways, at least.

I also began to seek out films that featured the Metro, my favourite being *Le Samouraï*, starring Alain Delon as an assassin whose pale face and blue eyes co-ordinate perfectly with the colour of Metro stations. It is quite impossible, by the way, to imagine Alain Delon on the London Underground.

I decided that knowledge of the Metro would give me purchase on Paris. We're talking about *savoir faire*, that important Parisian currency. 'Paris intimidates its visitors when it doesn't infuriate them,' writes Edmund White in *The Flâneur: A Stroll Through the Paradoxes of Paris*, 'but behind both sentiments dwells a sneaking suspicion that maybe the French have got it right, that they have located the *juste milieu*, and that their particular blend of artistic modishness and cultural conservatism, of welfare-statism and intense individualism, of clear-eyed realism and sappy romanticism – that these proportions are wise, time-tested and as indisputable as they are subtle.'

That was my own view, but I could never enjoy Paris unless I had a response to Parisian intimidation, and while I could never take on the city itself, I could take on the Metro. I would become an underground flâneur, secretly aiming to know more about the Metro than the average Parisian, and there did seem to be an opening here, because most of the authors I enjoyed reading on Paris never mentioned the Metro; there seemed a conspiracy of silence about it.

The best-known Metro novel is *Zazie Dans Le Metro* (1959) by Raymond Queneau – charmingly filmed under that name in 1960 – whose central joke is that Zazie, who has worshipped the Metro from afar – that is, from the French provinces – doesn't get to ride on it during her trip to Paris, because of a strike. And I had been reading Georges Simenon's novels featuring Inspector Maigret for years before it occurred to me that, despite living and working in Paris and being apparently unable to drive a car, he never seemed to take the Metro. It turns out he does take it, but rarely, and he doesn't like it. A November 2006 article by Murielle Wenger on trussel.com, which is dedicated to Simenon and other matters likely to interest readers of this book, such as Metro maps, gives chapter and verse. 'The Metro, it's true, is the fastest method of locomotion,' Wenger writes. 'But Maigret is not a man of speed; he had need of all his ponderousness, of his slow rumination to bring his cases to a successful termination.' She gives examples. From 'Death of a Nobody', a short story collected in *Maigret's Christmas:* 'the Metro, which smelled of bleach and where Maigret had to put out his pipe'. (Maigret could smoke on Parisian buses if he stood on the rear platform.)

In *Quartet* (1928) by Jean Rhys, a novel steeped in Parisian practicalities, the characters always take trams, for heaven's sake, even though trams were no cheaper. And here is Ernest Hemingway, sidestepping the Metro in his memoir of 1920s Paris, *A Movable Feast*: 'I would walk along the *quais* when I finished work ... There were many ways of walking down to the river from the top of Cardinal Lemoine.' Did he know that Line 7 went the same way? Of his colleagues from the literary 'lost generation', we must be grateful to Ezra Pound for having deigned to notice the Metro, or the people on it, as described in his two-line poem (which I assume would be expensive to quote, any part of it constituting a large part), 'In a Station of the Metro'. It has been much discussed, sometimes cited as the quintessential Imagist poem. My own prosaic contribution would be to mention that, according to Pound's own recollection (mentioned in Volume 1 of *Ezra Pound: Poet*, by A. David Moody), it describes a scene at Concorde station, where he saw a succession of beautiful faces.

George Orwell was very interested in the London Underground, in the sense that he hated it for its promotion of the commuting lifestyle, but he has nothing to say about the Underground, and very little about the Metro, in *Down and Out in Paris and London* (1933). He did occasionally use Line 6 for the twenty-minute ride from his lodgings near Place d'Italie to Cambronne, near the restaurant where he worked as a *plongeur*, or washer-up. This would have taken him over an elevated section, but if that lifted his spirits, he doesn't mention it. In the mornings, he 'fought for a place on the Metro'. He finished work at half past midnight when he might accept a glass of brandy from the patron. Then, 'As a rule the last Metro was almost empty – a great advantage, for one could sit down and sleep for a quarter of an hour.' He did feel that every Metro fare was a waste of one franc fifty, but it might be that descriptions of Metro or Underground rides were at odds with his 'down and out' persona.

Marcel Proust never went on a Metro train, despite the engrossing chapter in Graham Robb's *Parisians: An Adventure History of Paris* headed 'Marcel in the Metro'. It's a bit of a *Zazie Dans Le Metro* situation, in that for Proust the Metro 'might as well have been a fantasy by H. G. Wells' – this even though from 1906 he lived on boulevard Haussmann, 'less than 300 yards from the Saint Lazare Metro station'. In August 1906, Proust did spend 'two hours wheezing' in Saint-Lazare main-line station while trying – and failing – to muster the strength to descend to the Metro to travel to Père Lachaise for his uncle's funeral. (Of course, Proust would reach Père Lachaise eventually, in 1922.)

Proust does mention the Metro in *Sodom and Gomorrah*, volume four of *In Search of Lost Time*. On 30 January 1918, he had perhaps witnessed, from the back of his chauffeur-driven car, Parisians seeking shelter in Metro stations from a bombing raid; he certainly read of it in the next day's newspaper. His imagination then took over. 'Some of those Pompeians, as the fire of heaven rained down on them, descended into the corridors of the Metro, knowing that they would not be alone there; and the darkness that irradiates everything like a new element abolishes the first phase of pleasure and offers direct access to a domain of caresses that is normally attained only after a certain length of time.'

It seemed I admired the Metro more than most Parisians, and that made me even keener on it: I was sticking up for the

underdog. Of course, I only ever saw the Metro in optimal circumstances: that is, while on some kind of holiday, and usually
travelling during the off-peak. I have lived in Paris for brief
periods, but never had to commute there, never had to tangle
with that world-weary Parisian jingle: *'Metro, Boulot, Dodo'*
('Metro, work, sleep', which is an abbreviation of a line of a
poem, 'Couleurs d'Usine', by Pierre Béarn). But it did seem to
me that Parisians were ungrateful for what they'd been given.
I've just been reading Christine Féret-Fleury's novel *The Girl
Who Reads on the Metro*, in which the central character seeks
to escape a life of nine-to-five drudgery. The book opens with
an evocation of her daily journey to work on the Metro – on
the 'ordinary' days: 'days when the stops, warning signals and
clanging were regular, the days that weren't exceptionally
overcrowded, when there weren't any accidents, terror alerts
or strikes, and no unscheduled stops to regulate the service.
Ordinary days. The days when you feel as though you're a cog
in a well-oiled machine.'

Now this daily journey takes place on the above-mentioned
elevated section of Metro Line 6, where I always feel as
if I'm flying. At one point the character exits from one of
these elevated stations (not her usual stop), and the only
acknowledgement of its situation is that she is quickly in the
surrounding streets. If the story had been set on the deeply
buried, murky Northern Line of the London Underground, the
character would probably have been fighting her way to the
surface along crowded corridors and up overloaded escalators.
Even on the cover of *The Girl Who Reads on the Metro* – which

is an enjoyable novel, by the way – Line 6 looks attractive as it heads into a blur of golden light: sunset or sunrise, the line running broadly east–west.

Not only have I never commuted in Paris; I have also never spent any long period of time in its less glamorous suburbs, and I ought to concede that the Metro has long been an elitist railway. It has served Paris, and its two million relatively prosperous residents, far more effectively than it has the relatively less prosperous ten million who live in the other seven *départements* of the Île de France region. By 'Paris' here, I mean Paris proper, which is the territory bounded by the most recent of the defensive walls that denote the history of the city like the rings of a tree trunk: the Thiers Wall, which was built in the 1840s and demolished at a leisurely pace between the end of the First World War and 1932. Paris proper counts as a single *commune* – the largest one in France. It is also a *département.* All other French *départements* include many communes; the *département* of Paris only the one – and I'm afraid we are not quite done with the neurotic intricacies of French local government.

The Metro serves the suburbs of Paris less well than the Underground serves those in London. Harrow, say, which is in Greater London, 13 miles from the centre, has an Underground station. People living in Noisy-le-Grand, a *commune* 9 miles from the centre of Paris in the *département* of Seine-Saint-Denis, do not, at the time of writing, have a Metro station, but Paris is about to embrace its near neighbours.

Noisy-le-Grand is one of the 123 *communes* within the three *départements* of the 'Petit-Couronne', or 'small ring' – a term denoting the *départements* immediately bordering Paris, and these are to be joined with Paris (and seven other outer-suburban *communes*) in a new administrative body called the Metropolis of Grand Paris, which was created in 2016, the outcome of a vision for Paris and its neighbours first enunciated by Nicolas Sarkozy in 2007. So there will be a Greater Paris, just as there is a Greater London. Many ambitious construction and regeneration schemes aimed at 'territorial rebalancing' have been inaugurated by the Metropolis. There is also a parallel project being undertaken by a different body, the Society of Grand Paris, and this is a vast 35-billion-euro expansion of the Metro called Grand Paris Express. The centrepiece will be a new, orbital line – Line 15 – whose primary role is not to connect the suburbs to Paris in the old, condescending, radial way: it will connect the suburbs to *each other*, although there will also be radial connections to it, by extensions to existing Metro lines, and there will be a station to serve Noisy on Line 15.

In addition, there will be two other, outer orbital lines, numbered 16 and 18, which, on the map of the GPE, are like handles placed either side of the central circle – imagine the steering wheel of a racing car. Line 17 will head off tangentially from Line 16 to Charles de Gaulle Airport north-east of Paris. Construction of the Grand Paris Express began in 2016; it is scheduled to be completed in 2030 and, this being France with its great dirigiste energy, it probably will be. (The early Metro was built at lightning speed, and by a man whose name *meant* lightning, as we will see.)

With that in mind, the Metro evoked in this book may well

become known in years to come as 'the classic Metro' or 'Metro. 01'. But I think this original network will be spoken of with affection (even by Parisians), despite its history of exclusivity, because it is a beautiful thing, just as the Grand Paris Express will be, and it is significant that the new lines are going to be branded as part of the Metro rather than as part of the RER, the Réseau Express Régional, big brother of the Metro, which serves the suburbs more comprehensively than the Metro, but lacks the Metro's glamour. I think of that as a real-world railway, as opposed to the delicate tracery of the Metro, which serves the fantasy-land of Paris proper.

I hope that, as a foreigner, I will be allowed some other indulgencies or liberties by any French readers. For instance, I've spoken of the North and South Banks of Paris, because to call them the Left and Right Banks seems perverse when you look at the actual map. (The logic is that they are on the left and right in relation to the flow of the Seine.) And, even given that I am English, French readers or speakers might find too little French in this book and too much English. I have tended to translate into English and, with all due respect to the e-acute in 'Métro' as written in French, I have left it out. To my English eyes, it would be too cluttering, and besides, the accent has usually been omitted from Metro station signs.

The title of this introduction is a translation of *'Chers voyageurs'* – the pleasingly formal way in which the travelling public are addressed on Metro announcements. It does sound, and look, better in French, of course, so I have adopted '*voyageurs*' for regular use in the pages that follow, but I don't like it when presumably bilingual English authors quote big chunks of French without translating. They're usually just showing off, knowing their readers will be too ashamed to complain that they couldn't understand. (By the way, I'd much rather think of myself as a '*voyageur*' than a 'customer', which is what I am on the London Underground.)

I'm not bilingual, to say the least, even after a year of being badgered by the emails of Duolingo. I can read French slightly better than I can speak it, and I was once informed, by a French person, that I had 'the accent from hell'. Part of the reason I'm intimidated by the French is that they can *speak* French, surely a sadistically difficult language, where you must learn not only the noun but also its gender – and how's that going to play out in an increasingly androgynous world, I'd like to know? And why is 'Metro' masculine? The Paris Metro, by the slightness and delicacy of its forms, its chicness and fashion-consciousness, is definitely feminine.

If I do display a lack of *savoir faire* and too much gaucherie in what follows, I hope I will be forgiven, because this book is, after all, a billet-doux addressed to the most stylish railway network in the world: the Paris Metro.

I

FIRST IMPRESSIONS

First Memory – the Spragues

My Dad worked for British Rail, and we had concessionary travel on what was then called 'the Continent', so we would go by train to holiday resorts in Spain and Italy. This involved travelling first to Paris, the European sleeper train hub, and undertaking the potentially fraught 'change at Paris'. In the case of the British, this usually involved transferring from Gare du Nord to the southerly and sun-facing Gare de Lyon. We once attempted the transfer by taxi and missed our connection – I still remember Dad sweating in the cab. Of course, the stakes are always high when approaching Gare de Lyon, as they would be on a date with someone beautiful. ('When one smells the hot transformer-oil of the Gare de Lyon', Bryan Morgan wrote in 1955 in *The End of the Line: A Book About Railways and Places, Mainly Continental*, 'one smells, behind, all the spaces of the *terre majeure* spreading in the sun.')

I remember doing it several times by Metro, and I wish I could remember those times better. From Gare du Nord, we would probably have taken Line 4 south to Châtelet, before taking Line 1 west to Gare de Lyon. Back then – in the mid-1970s – Châtelet Metro station was not yet a mere annex to the great railway complex of Châtelet Les Halles, which is primarily a station of the RER. (Châtelet Les Halles, by the way, was still under construction in the mid-1970s, manifesting as the largest hole ever dug in middle of a capital city, a hole big – and arid – enough for a western to have been filmed there: *Touche Pas à la Femme Blanche*, starring Catherine Deneuve.)

But I think that sometimes we accidentally veered off Lines 1 and 4, entering even more unfamiliar territory. I recall Dad having to carry our two suitcases down some stairs, because the Metro, being shallow, usually thinks it can get away with offering stairs rather than escalators. I had the impression of the train rocketing bad-temperedly into the hot station: a series of green, clattering steel boxes, scattering sparks – electrical and mechanical – with coupling gear swinging about lewdly at the front and a sleazy-looking, off-centre red light. Surely this train's home station was Pigalle? It was dark green, of an elusive but definitely foreign shade. I think you could call it bamboo green, but it went well with the red light, and the train was attractive because of the honesty of the design.

The train belonged to what was called 'the Sprague-Thomson stock', or 'Sprague stock' for short, which represented the most refined version of multiple-unit train design available at the time – a multiple-unit being a train with power distributed along its length in power cars, which are combined with engine-less trailer cars. The Metro, unlike the London Underground, does not have many American influences, but the Sprague-Thomson name reflects American origins: the technology was developed by the Thomson-Houston Electric

Company and Frank J. Sprague. Multiple-unit traction was essential to the development of all metros, and when you consider that Sprague also developed elevator and escalator technology, you begin to see him as the father of modern urban life.

The all-metal Spragues replaced the first generation of Metro stock, which were wooden, and the successive iterations of the Spragues are considered the classic Metro stock because of their longevity (1908 to 1983) and because they looked, and sounded, so excitingly primitive. Much of the equipment was on the outside, to keep it cool in the tunnels; the seats were mainly bare wood; lighting was by strings of 40-watt bulbs. You can see Spragues in action in *Last Tango in Paris*, which is a great Metro film, as well as catering to other, less wholesome predilections. The torrid exchanges between Marlon Brando and Maria Schneider are punctuated by shots of Spragues thundering along the viaduct carrying Line 6 across central-south Paris. You can see a Sprague car imprisoned behind glass in the lobby of the RATP headquarters – Maison de la RATP – on the Quai de la Rapée, where it is viewable by the public during office hours.

Even amid the stress of having to get to the Gare de Lyon on time, Dad set the suitcases down on the platform of a junction station where we changed lines, to commend to us that there were only two exits: 'Correspondance' (if you wanted to change to any number of other lines) and 'Sortie'. On the London Underground there would have been exits for every connecting line – not so elegant, you see. Dad was a railway

Francophile, like a character in *The Permanent Way*, David Hare's play of 2003 about the privatisation of British Rail. 'Why can the French do it?' asks the unnamed protagonist. 'I was brought up to believe the French couldn't do anything. But they can run a railway.' In the 1970s BR was in retrenchment mode and, for Dad, France was a place where railways were valued at their true worth as public utilities; hence high investment (the TGV network was being created at the time) and cheap fares. Paris, then and now, is the public transport city par excellence, but Europeans generally have a better commitment to public transport than the British. As a senior manager on the London Underground once told me, the discrepancy is down to our uniquely stratified class system: 'We think trains and buses are for people who can't afford cars.'

The Sprague livery was green of various dark shades, turning silver-grey later on. The green-ness of the early Metro trains would have seemed logical to Parisians, since that was also the colour of Metro station fixtures: ticket and telephone booths, railings and *portillons* (gates or barriers at platform entrances). Green was also the colour of municipal Paris above ground, chiefly to harmonise with the many street trees. Parisian buses used to be green, and the domed Parisian Morris columns – which are like lightning conductors for advertising posters, being designed to receive them and so keep them off the house walls – still are. Despite looking oriental, these epitomise Paris, and they survive in the traditional way in the poorer arrondissements, but with electronic screens in the smarter ones. Parisian benches and pissoirs (the latter gone now) were also green, as were the drinking fountains – Wallace Fountains, donated by a philanthropic Englishman, these latter two operating, so to speak, hand in hand. The botanical-looking Art Nouveau Metro entrances by Hector Guimard (about which we will be having more to say) were also green, albeit of a paler shade, that of weathered copper. Admittedly, the dominant colour scheme of post-Sprague trains of various types was a rich blue and cream, but that was still part of the Metro palette, since the station signs were blue and white. Further shades of grey intervened thereafter, but Metro trains have always looked good, and we are back to green with some of the current ones: the jade green of the operator, RATP.

The Apparent Speed of the Trains

Subsequent Metro trains have lacked the charisma of the jangling Spragues, but they do have a certain presence, especially if you're British. They are about the same width as trains on the deep-level parts of the Underground (the Tubes) but taller, appearing tall and thin, like the trams of which they are close cousins. It's ironic that it should be the London Underground that ended up with trains the shape of baguettes. You instinctively crouch on the London Tube; Metro trains encourage you to stand tall – one reason why they're less claustrophobic.

They appear to come bustling into the stations like tall, officious maiden aunts (and maiden aunts in slippers, in the case of the trains with tyres). They stop peremptorily, then scurry out again, seeming very impatient, which is partly an illusion. Metro trains are in fact generally slower than those on the London Underground; they don't need to be so fast because Metro stations are closer together (on average only 500 metres apart) than Underground stations. But they seem exhilaratingly faster, because of rapid acceleration and deceleration, especially on the lines where the trains are *'matériel pneu'* – that is, with tyres on their wheels, as opposed to *'matériel fer'* (steel wheels). Peak-hour service intervals on the Metro are shorter than those on the London Underground, and the Parisians are well drilled at quick alighting and boarding. Everyone seems to know the precise moment at which the train becomes too crowded to justify sitting on one of the folding seats near the doors, the *strapontins*: the occupants of these rise to their feet in unison, like people giving a standing ovation in the theatre, and on most Metro carriages the seat promptly snaps back upright behind them. I pride myself on joining in this seat-relinquishment the moment it occurs – although I was once guilt-tripped into standing only after noticing that the man next to me, who had been about to tuck into a packed lunch arrayed on his lap, had done so. (There are notices reminding *voyageurs* not to use the seats when the train is crowded, and on one of my first visits to Paris I mistranslated *'en case d'affluence'* as 'in case of flatulence'. I couldn't quite see the logic of the injunction.)

On the older Metro stocks, the *voyageur* gets to open the door him- or herself, whether to get out or in. This is done either by pressing a green button or, on the still older trains, by employing a winding motion to lift a steel latch called a *loqueteau*, whereupon the double doors spring violently apart as if they'd always hated each other. In one of the many ridiculous chase scenes in the film *Fear Over the City* (1975), Jean-Paul Belmondo, as a pursuing policeman, shoots a villain on a Line 6 Metro train; the villain falls against the door to somehow accidentally activate the *loqueteau* and tumble out into the path of an approaching train. A *loqueteau* can't be opened accidentally, of course: that's the whole point of the design; it's quite hard to open one *deliberately*, and I'm always slightly nervous if I'm the one nearest a door of this type, with a mob of impatient Parisians mustered behind me. If I don't fumble the procedure, I feel disproportionately chuffed — honoured to have been entrusted with the task. But on occasion, when I have been the only person wanting to get off a crowded train arriving at a minority interest station, the Parisians have let me down. Under stress, my French is not up to requesting that someone nearer the door open it for me and I have missed my stop.

On occasion, London Underground passengers have been able to open the doors themselves, but all doors on the Underground currently open automatically. One advantage of letting the passengers open the doors themselves is that heat is retained in carriages no-one wants to alight from or board, but that's only an advantage in winter. A reason *not* to let them control the doors is that it's expensive to maintain the individual latches. We have hit another of those 'cultural differences' between the Metro and the Underground. In his learned afterword to the highly cerebral *In the Metro* by the French

ethnologist Marc Augé, Tom Conley writes of the *loqueteaux*
that they 'require a minimal but decisive gesture, reminding
everyone that he or she lives in an unflinchingly post-Sartrian
world in which "being for oneself" is felt when we open the
door by our own decision'. (London, it seems, then, is not in the
'post-Sartrian' world.)

In the film *Le Samouraï*, about which we will have more to
say, Alain Delon evades his pursuer by flipping the *loqueteau* to
alight from a Metro train the second before its departure – a
trope repeated many times in film scenes on other networks,
but particularly suited to the all-action Metro.

The White Vaults

As a boy, I was struck by the elemental nature and coherence
of the Metro. It is styled in a way the London Underground is
not; there is a unified vision. Whereas the Underground is a
TV series, the Metro is a feature film. The vision was particularly clear immediately after the inauguration of the system
in 1900. In the stations, there were only really two colours:
white and blue – the white of the tiles, the dark blue of the
signs on which the station names were written in white. The
white tiles had bevelled edges, to reflect as much as possible
of the low-wattage electric light. In early photos of the Metro,
nobody's reading a book, because that wasn't possible in the
available light, but such light as existed created a moonlight-
on-the sea effect over those bevelled tiles, and the elegance of

the stations was commensurate with that of the streets above. The pallor of Haussmann's boulevards was the equivalent of the white Metro tiling; the street signs were in blue and white, like the Metro signs.

Even the spaces between the stations – that is, the tunnels – are visually enjoyable, certainly more so than those of the London Underground, most of which are literal 'tubes', or 'pipes' to the railway professionals. It's true that while 57 per cent of the London Underground is above ground, only 8 per cent of the Metro is, but when a London Underground train is in one of the pipes, the carriage windows are superfluous. There is nothing to see but the dark and dirty tunnel wall rolling past a few inches away. Every so often there is a light, but you can't see its approach: it just slides past, seemingly illuminating nothing but itself.

The Tubes are deep-level lines, buried at least 40 feet down in the London clay that is so accommodating to tunnels of that type. Luckily for users of its subterranean railway, Paris is not built on clay. Its geology is heterogeneous.

Paris is also riddled with the workings of old limestone and gypsum quarries, particularly in the north-east, and wherever possible the Metro avoided all these complications by staying close to the surface, like those early London Underground tunnels that are not the Tubes: the sub-surface lines, principally the Metropolitan and District, which had to be shallow because when they were built, in the 1860s, they had to accommodate steam trains, and so needed to be close to the open air for ventilation.

The tunnel roofs created for the Met and District in London were, like those of the Paris Metro, usually elliptical; that is, vaulted – a harmonious and pleasant outcome. On the Metropolitan Railway, the *stations* often had no roof, or at least not a stone one. It was cheaper to do without, and stone roofs only inhibited the ventilation the steam trains required. A station might be left open to the air, occupying a great gash in the ground, as at Edgware Road; or it might be skimpily roofed over with glass, as at Notting Hill. The Parisians didn't want their stations to obtrude in this blister-like way; there was neither the space nor the taste for it. So the Metro stations were roofed over, usually with the same elliptical roofs as the tunnels except wider, whereas on the Metropolitan Railway, the only station with a complete stone elliptical roof was Baker Street, which was consequently the most beautiful one on the line, and such a novelty that parties of Victorian schoolchildren were taken to see it.

At this point, I would like to introduce my friend, Julian Pepinster, who had an English father and a French mother, and who lives in a stylish flat in the 6th Arrondissement decorated with Metro posters and model Metro trains. Julian is president of an organisation called ADEMAS (Association d'Exploitation du Matériel Sprague), which celebrates the Sprague stock and Metro history generally. He is the author of a highly regarded book on the system, *Le Metro de Paris*. Julian also works for the Metro – in 'internal security' he says, intimidatingly, and with his lean build and shaved head he does look like a commando. But his approach to the Metro is poetic. Despite working on it, he travels on the system to unwind. He told me that he 'loves the ambience'; he also suggested to me that 'a Metro station vault is like the wine cellar of a château, which is a very nice thing to be reminded of.'

The vault is the key to the elegance of the Metro. It has all sorts of knock-on benefits. It is wide enough to accommodate two platforms facing each other with two tracks in between, compared to one track and one platform in a Tube station. It's more sociable to have facing platforms. You will see – and hear – two Parisians continuing late-night conversations by shouting across the platforms even after they have diverged to go in opposite directions. And the two tracks allow the trains to run companionably side-by-side (albeit in opposite directions), whereas one tube tunnel accommodates one train: a rat-in-a-drainpipe effect. I have begun to experience claustrophobia on crowded Tube trains (a strange fate to befall someone who's written two books about the system), but I never feel claustrophobic on the Metro. This is because there is lateral space either side of the trains which you can actually *see*, Metro tunnels being illuminated – quite dimly, but sufficiently for the purposes of graffiti artists. (The tunnel lights occur at slightly irregular heights, as if held up by disparate individuals in a torchlight procession.) The roominess of the tunnels also permits most Metro trains to have openable windows, which again relieves claustrophobia. You can't have openable windows on tube trains because the tunnel wall is too close. Anyone sticking any part of their anatomy through them would be at risk of injury, and the onrush of air would be noisy. Openable windows are also not compatible with air-conditioning, which is why British railwaymen's slang for air-conditioned trains is 'coffins'. Metro trains, like the deep-level Tubes of the Underground, are not formally air-conditioned, but they are better cooled than the Tubes, and by a variety of methods: refrigerated air, mechanical fans or vents in the roof.

There have been departures from the white vault template, and we will be discussing those. But since the beginning of the Renouveau du Metro programme in 1999, the Metro has recommitted to white bevelled tiles and that early, simple sparkle. So Paris is 'the city of light', even underground.

Station Entrances

London Underground stations almost all have surface buildings. The ones that don't – Chancery Lane, Vauxhall, Warwick Avenue, for instance – seem bereft, denied their true inheritance. The Underground, unlike the Metro, is deep, and surface buildings were required to house lifts, hence the oxblood-tiled (or bruise-coloured) Edwardian station buildings of Leslie Green, which have tall ground floors and a mezzanine above for the lift gear. There are about forty of these across central London, and it is impossible to imagine the Paris city authority allowing the Metro to colonise the streets in the same manner, even if the system had required as many lifts as the London Underground. Paris was already, in effect, a conservation zone as early as 1900 when the Metro opened.

The Metro did need to advertise itself, however, and it would do so by commissioning Hector Guimard, the star of the fashionable Art Nouveau movement, to design station entrances that seem to British eyes both skimpy (since no surface building was usually involved) and outrageous. The commonest type of Guimard entrance or *'entourage'* takes the form of a cast-iron railing bounding three sides of a Metro staircase and decorated with vine motifs and cartouches reminiscent of large turtle shells. Sprouting from this railing – in most cases – are two iron sculptures of monstrous plants, of no known genus (except perhaps triffid), with lamps where the flowers would be. The closest real-life equivalent is lily of the valley, and if you bought two of those from a garden centre and placed them side by side, so that when their flowers blossomed they bowed towards each other, you would have grown your own miniature Guimard entrance. Lily of the valley flowers are white, and the Guimard lamps are also white until they are illuminated (which might happen in the middle of a drizzly winter's afternoon, if the station supervisor below decides conditions are sufficiently gloomy), whereupon they glow either red or orange in a diabolic way, which is why – to move from flora to fauna – they have been compared to dragons' eyes. They are also suggestive of eyes on stalks, such as a snail's.

The Guimard flowers are midnight ramblers, coming alive when illuminated. In daylight, the fantasy doesn't quite take off: it's like seeing a nightclub in the daytime. But the magic is always latent in them, and they look as compellingly bizarre today as they did in 1900.

Station Names

One of the first aspects of Metro history I read up on was station names, and it was a pleasure to read about them, just as it was a pleasure to read the names themselves on the Metro map. I was in any case predisposed towards the subject because it preoccupied my favourite historian of France, Richard Cobb, whose droll and dreamy style once prompted an admiring reviewer to describe him as 'a sort of Betjeman in a beret', and for whom the Metro was 'the most poetical form of Parisian transport'. When discussing the Metro, he habitually invoked the advertising slogan 'Dubo, Dubon, Dubonnet', which accompanied an image of a little man taking on by degrees the colour of that aperitif as he drained his glass in one go – and as the colour was dark red, you wouldn't have thought this a transformation many people would have sought. Cobb referred to the image as 'flickering' (a word he was very keen on), but the image can't have been animated; presumably it seemed to flicker as the trains entered or left the stations where it appeared. Cobb was a visiting fellow at my Oxford college, and I met him on a couple of occasions; he was a small man, impish in appearance and character, and generally flushed with red wine. In fact, he could have been the Dubonnet Man incarnate.

In 'Itineraries', an essay in his collection *Paris and Elsewhere*, Cobb writes of Metro station names as being like 'old friends', even if they are occasionally grandiose: 'it is hard to take Filles du Calvaire seriously, Sèvres-Babylone poses no threat, Solférino, Chambre des Députés, as seen from below ground, are entirely unprestigious.' The latter, located on Line 12 behind the Musée d'Orsay, is less unprestigious now. In 1989 the station was renamed Assemblée Nationale to reflect the new name of the chamber. The vault is lined with steel, on which slogans in praise of democracy are decoratively inscribed; the proceedings of the chamber are showed on slightly blurred and bluish TV screens, the fraught debates at odds with the harmony of the Metro. As for Filles du Calvaire (the 'Daughters of Calvary'), it's named after a nearby convent − well, it was nearby in the eighteenth century − and while the *voyageur* emerging from that station's undistinguished exit finds him- or herself on the workaday boulevard du Temple in the 11th Arrondissement, the poetically conceived rotunda of the Cirque d'Hiver is within sight, and it resembles a great wedding cake when illuminated at night.

In his earlier book *Promenades*, Cobb had described 'the sheer extraordinary juxtaposition of names, Sèvres-Babylone, Les Filles du Calvaire, Barbes Rochechouart, which has got such an extraordinary sort of *chuintement* about it, particularly when pronounced by a Parisian'. (*Chuintement* means 'hiss'.) Cobb spoke of the 'poesy' of the Metro station names, and Clive James was so entranced by the name of one station, Porte des Lilas (Gate of Lilacs), that he applied it to his long poem about Marcel Proust, in which he encourages his readers to learn French, adding that it will be enriching, even if you don't 'Get enough French to travel on the Metro'.

Others might think the Metro names are less poetic than prolix. Somebody once attempted to underline this point by telling me that only three Metro stations have four-letter names: Rome, Iéna, Cité and Haxo, the latter being not so much a closed-down as a never-opened station. (We will be visiting Haxo.) This seemed telling, until I realised that only *two* Underground stations have four-letter names: Bank and Oval. Nonetheless, the Metro *is* prolix, but enjoyably so, for the most part.

Most of its station names are derived from a nearby street, or a pair of them. Parisians are proud of their streets, so they'd rather namecheck two than one, and double-barrelled names pinpoint a station's location, giving its precise co-ordinates, as in a game of battleships, which is useful given the density of stations. Examples are Marcadet Poissoniers (Lines 4 and 12) or Maubert Mutualité (Line 10). There are also some three-part names, perhaps created by the addition of a subtitle. In 1998 Saint Denis-Porte de Paris on Line 13 became Saint Denis-Porte de Paris-Stade de France, when the stadium opened in that year. There is also Boulogne-Pont de Saint Cloud (Rhin et Danube) on Line 10, and Bobigny-Pablo Picasso (Préfecture-Hôtel du Département) on Line 5. It's just as well that, even in the days when tickets might be bought over a counter, *voyageurs* seldom had to *say* the name of a station, since the fare was the same to all of them.

'The Metro is above all a system of names,' writes Lawrence Osborne in his *Paris Dreambook*: 'names which are a thousand times more secretive than the places they supposedly denote.'

Bryan Morgan, novelist and railway buff, makes the same point in *The End of the Line*. The Metro, he writes, 'provides the most magical things in Paris with its station names. Sèvres Babylone, Réaumur-Sebastapol, Pyramides, La Motte-Picquet-Grenelle, Porte des Lilas ... These are places where the fancy can flicker about what *ought* to be overhead, though experience knows that it is only the same old square with the same tall mansarded houses, the same old buses with the same vermouth advertisements.' Morgan, too, has a thing about Dubonnet: 'DUBO-DUBON-DUBONNET over and over, monotonous as Paris itself.' (Like most people who don't like Paris, by the way, Morgan makes it sound attractive even as he criticises it.)

Lawrence Osborne agrees with Richard Cobb in picking out Filles du Calvaire as being over-the-top, but also 'Bel-Air, Crimée, Danube, Pyramides, Campo-Formio, Botzaris, Croix-de-Chavaux, Jasmin, Ourcq ... the mercurial names of the Metro, with the exoticism of the names of extinct birds and buried cities'. Mercurial in the sense of mysterious, but also in the sense of being likely to change. Some of the names are international, therefore subject to fluctuating international relations. Berlin (on what is now Line 13) closed in August 1914 and re-opened in 1916 as Liège, and the street after which it was named underwent the same change. Also in 1916, Allemagne on Line 2 was renamed Jaurès after an assassinated socialist politician.

On Line 10, Wilhelm, named, innocently enough, after an Alsatian poet, nonetheless became Église d'Auteuil in 1921. In

1946, what had been Marbeuf-Rond Point des Champs Élysées
on Lines 1 and 9 was named Franklin D. Roosevelt, and seven
stations were named after Resistance heroes, including the two
Corentins (Corentin Celton on Line 12 and Corentin Cariou on
Line 7); the station called Combat on Line 12 became Colonel
Fabien. Fabien, real name Pierre Georges, had shot a German
naval cadet at Barbes Rochechouart station in 1941, for which
hundreds of Parisians would pay with their lives. Stalingrad
station, located near the Place de la Bataille de Stalingrad, commemorates the battle victory of the Red Army in 1943. I own a
DVD simply called *Paris Metro*, which consists of footage taken
in 1976 and 1987 by John Laker, who also provides the commentary and obviously objects to the Red Army being feted: 'Is
this station due for a name change?' he grumbles, over the first
clip showing Stalingrad. He returns to the station later on with
a sarcastic 'The viewer can be assured we are still in Paris.'

Many stations are named after Napoleonic battles
(Austerlitz, Pyramides, Iéna and Wagram) or Napoleonic
generals (Cambronne, Daumesnil, Duroc, Kléber, Mouton-
Duvernet, Pelleport). But no station is called Napoleon.
'Incredible self-effacement', writes Osborne, given that there's
a station named after George V, and another after Garibaldi.
But having a Metro station named after you can be a hostage
to fortune. Many Anglophone tourists in search of naughtiness
have no doubt subconsciously assumed that Pigalle is named
after some porcine pornographer; in fact, it commemorates –
or traduces the memory of – Jean-Baptiste Pigalle (1714–85),
sculptor of the Winged Venus, which has pride of place at the

top of the monumental Daru staircase in the Louvre, where it aspires to all that Pigalle (the place) is not.

In his *Paris Metro Handbook*, Brian Hardy points out that some names disappeared only to reappear later. On Line 3, rue Saint-Denis became Réaumer-Sébastopol in 1907 (the name-changing getting underway only seven years after the network opened), but 'Saint-Denis' reappeared as Boulevard Saint-Denis on Line 4 in 1908 and appeared again in 1976 when Line 13 reached the suburban town of Saint-Denis.

I once sat in on a discussion of why Southwark Station, opened in 1999 on the Jubilee Line Extension of the London Underground, was so called. Some locals had wanted it to be called Paris Gardens (a prettier name, they thought), but LU, displaying a very un-Parisian prudishness, objected that the Gardens in question had once been known as a red-light zone. Other locals had favoured Bankside, after the nearby power station, which is now Tate Modern. LU rejected this as supposedly too similar to the name of Bank Station. The London Underground does have some name clashes – think of all those Claphams – but there are more in Paris. Sèvres appears three times, as Sèvres Babylone (10 and 12) and Pont de Sèvres (Line 9) and Sèvres Lecourbe (Line 6). On Line 10, there are only two stops between Michel-Ange Auteuil and Michel-Ange Molitor ('Michel-Ange' being Michelangelo), but they are on a loop, which is perhaps an excuse, because in such cases there is bound to be a certain corralling of nearby place names.

The Metro's prolixity reflects a deep consciousness of history.

The names of streets, after which the stations are named, are often explained by further blue and white signs along them, so that Paris seems graveyard-like, full of memorials and inscriptions. In this way Père Lachaise and Montparnasse Cemeteries, where the tombs are set in walkable signposted rows, are Paris in microcosm.

Direction

For me, the Metro started where Eurostar ended, at Gare du Nord station on Line 4, and it is time to mention that important Metro word, 'Direction', because the Metro is signposted by phrases like 'Direction Porte de Clignancourt' or 'Direction Bagneaux', those being the two termini of Line 4. If London used the same method, we'd have signs on the Northern Line reading, say, 'Direction High Barnet' or 'Direction Morden'. Instead, we say 'Northbound' or 'Southbound', or 'Westbound' and 'Eastbound' in the case of a line like the Central. But these terms are American, much of the London Underground having been built with American capital, and indeed *by* Americans, principally the transport visionary, and criminal, Charles Tyson Yerkes, who'd served time in the States for fraud. Other American terms used on the Underground were 'conductors' and 'cars' for carriages ('Move down inside the cars'). But Paris is more possessive of its Metro than London is of the Underground, so American terminology is largely shunned.

It follows that, to navigate the Metro, you need to know the names of the stations at the ends of the lines, which is problematic for several reasons. A system of navigation relying on the end points of the lines might have been fine in the case of a fairly static network like the Underground, but the Metro is not static: new stations keep being added, and they are added at the ends.

The early Metro terminated at the limits of Paris proper, defined, as we have seen, by the ghost of the Thiers Wall. The term 'Porte' in a Metro name – Porte des Lilas, for example – refers to a former gate in that wall, but from the 1930s onward, the Metro has pushed beyond Paris proper. The consequence is that on the line maps (*'plaques directionnelles'*) displayed on the approach to platforms, which list the stations coming up in the direction served by that particular platform (starting at the top with the station you're at) you will sometimes see a new terminus crudely added at the bottom, like a sticking plaster, ruining the purity of the sign. The stations are listed next to a depiction of the line in the line's colour, but until the 1990s, *plaques directionnelles* were just daunting lists of station names in white capitals on a blue background. (The white capital letters on the *plaques directionnelles* gave way in the late 1980s to more easy-going standard upper and lower case, and that is the style of the current typeface in use, designed by Jean Francois Porchez and called Parisine Bold.)

Another problem with 'Direction' is that there are a lot of lines to know the ends of. London's Underground has eleven lines, but there are fourteen on the Metro, or sixteen if you count those adjuncts 7*bis* and 3*bis*. (*'Bis'* is a funny little French word; I used to think it meant 'B', as in 221B Baker Street, but that can't be right, since there are no lines 7a and 3a. In fact, '*bis*' is a way of saying 'again' or 'more of the same'.) A friend of mine collects railway maps, and the one with pride of place in his house – framed on his kitchen wall – is a Paris Metro map from the 1970s. When I asked why, he said, 'Well, it was a present from my friend Patrice,' as though that were sufficient, which perhaps it was. But when I pressed him further, he said, 'Metro maps look better than Tube maps.' I pressed him again, and he said, 'They're more colourful because there are more lines.'

But that doesn't help with navigation: rather the reverse. The first-time visitor to Paris, needing to go north on Line 4 – 'Direction Clignancourt' – probably finds themselves tracing their fingers along the line on the map until they hit the edge of Paris, like children reading a comic and trying to solve one of those puzzles showing people holding fishing rods above a tangle of lines: 'Who has caught the big fish, and who has caught the tin can?' Paris novices were offered some relief from having to know the end points of the lines in 1937, with the appearance at many stations of backlit Metro maps: *plans indicateurs lumineux d'itinéraires* (PILI for short). You pressed the button for your destination station, and a route was suggested for you by a line of little lights. Few PILIs survive but, last time I looked, there was one at Miromesnil. I have used it myself; the sudden appearance of a glittering necklace is very gratifying, and you immediately press another station name at random for no reason except to see another necklace. There's another PILI at the entrance to Line 5 in the concourse beneath Gare du Nord, but it's out of action. The map survives, with every station a lightbulb, but the keypad is covered over with a board. You can prise this up slightly, to marvel at the controls once entrusted to public use – as small, silvery and closely spaced as the keys on an accordion.

During the first century of the Metro, the lines were hard to trace because the Metro map resembled a plate of linguine. It was not diagrammatised, like the London Underground map after Harry Beck had got his hands on it in 1932. Beck re-made the Underground map using only verticals, horizontals and 45-degree diagonals – a piece of cartographic genius, for which he was paid ten guineas, the equivalent in today's money of about £800. In 1939, Beck created a Metro map following his London rules, but when he submitted it, he was told it was 'not suitable for Paris'. It's true that he had tipped the angle of Line 1 quite severely for his main diagonal, and he took angular liberties with the river Seine, but Baron Haussmann had effected a geometric rationalisation of Paris every bit as ruthless as Harry Beck, and Haussmann had done it for real, not just on a piece of paper. Beck refined his Paris map in 1951. It's not known if he submitted this version, which is reproduced in Mark Ovenden's excellent book, *Paris Metro Style*. Ovenden writes that 'geometric distortions' are 'anathema to the French' because 'the shape of Paris is virtually engrained in the national psyche thanks to the struggles and insurrections of the people'. But in 2001, RATP capitulated to Beck's horizontals, verticals and diagonals (which have become orthodox around the world) with a map commissioned from the design agency BDC Conseil, and this remains the standard map concept.

The Metro map I most often used, even after 2001, dated from 1982, when the little *Plan de Paris* book in which it appeared was published. It had been a fold-out feature of the book, but some time in the late 1990s it had *fallen* out, and I carried it around separately. It was about the size of a silk pocket square (that is, not really big enough, once my eyesight had started to go), and it became so crumpled towards the end of its life that prior to tracing a 'direction' I would not so much unfold it as unpick it; and of course, it was out of date. Line 5 still terminated at Église de Pantin; Line 1 had not yet reached La Défense, and the Lines had not yet gained their modern colours, so Line 1 was black rather than 'buttercup', Line 5 was red, not orange – and Lines 4, 6 and 9 were also red, proving that you really did have to go by 'direction' and not colour.

The *Plan de Paris* books were published from the 1920s onward by two firms: Leconte and Guilmin. They had red or maroon covers that varied slightly over the years, but always carried the title *Plan de Paris par Arrondissement*, with the subtitle *'Avec la station de metro la plus proche'* ('With the nearest metro station shown'), all written in silvery Art Nouveau lettering, and sometimes with a silver star hovering nearby. The directory at the beginning listed all the streets, giving the places where they began and ended, the name of the nearest Metro station and a reference to the appropriate arrondissement maps, which occurred, in pretty colours, later on in the book. The *Plans de Paris* were very committed to the Metro, but when they mentioned the nearest station in the directory, its line number wasn't given, because both the number and the colour were subordinate to 'direction'. The books were very useful, nonetheless. They put the whole of Paris into your pocket. My wife had one of her own, an early Nineties edition, and her and my *Plans de Paris* would sit on the table between us when we met in a Paris café, just as people's mobile phones do now.

I'm not sure if the *Plans* are still being published in that form; I hope so. The newest one I can see on Amazon is dated 2011. It's a used copy and costs £27. There's an interesting essay about the books' history on the Francophile website, trussel.com.

City Limits

The Metro map is dense, because the Metro is dense, which brings us to some elemental facts. Paris proper (containing 2.2 million people) is only one of eight departments of the Île de France (containing nearly 12 million), and it is small: one-fifteenth the size of London. You can walk from north to south across Paris in two hours. It is small enough for me to have seen several of its major celebrities without trying: Catherine Deneuve drinking a coffee on a café terrace on rue de l'Odéon; Jane Birkin (English by birth, admittedly) filming near the pretty entrance to Lamarck-Caulaincourt station, which is bounded to either side by famous steps going up Montmartre hill. (Having previously interviewed her, I waved hopefully; she didn't appear to recognise me.)

Paris is also densely populated – four times more so than London – and most visitors experience Paris in cramped conditions. Hotel lifts are birdcage-like; toilets in a bar are usually just two closets. In 1887, the novelist Joris-Karl Huysmans complained of Baron Haussmann's rationalisation of the Paris streets that 'In the past the streets were narrow, and the apartments vast; now the streets are very wide, and the rooms are tiny and stuffy.' Parisian kitchens often don't have space for washing machines, hence all those 1950s-looking laundrettes about the place. My wife's flat, off rue Mouffetard, had a bath about 4 foot long. Nobody lives in a *house* in Paris, not even Mick Jagger, and the flats in the mansard roofs of the Haussmann blocks are celebrated for their compactness. Writing about these '*chambres de bonne*' for the *Daily Telegraph* in 1998, I interviewed a woman who had one for sale, and she was so confident of selling it that she didn't want me to publish her contact details. In *An American in Paris*, Gene Kelly plays (not very convincingly) a struggling artist who lives in a *chambre de bonne*. In the mornings – which in the film are always sunny – he winds his narrow bed up to the ceiling on a pulley. His collapsible dining table has the dimensions of a milk crate.

At first sight, the Metro also seems small. When standing on a Metro station platform, you can often see the next station, a little island of light a few hundred yards along the tunnel, the people there looking just like the people around you. On

Line 12, for instance, you can see Assemblée Nationale from Solférino, and vice versa.

A station entrance might be just a staircase, an exit a small escalator that seems out of order, but if you call its bluff by stepping on it, you will trip the photo-electric sensor and it will start moving and carry you up, and not very far up, as a rule, the Metro being so shallow. Most London Underground escalators flow continuously, with the complacency of a waterfall, regardless of whether anyone is nearby. London Underground has been known for its many escalators and its many *broken* escalators, and the assumption is that any passengers seeing a stationary one will assume it's in that category. Paris is coming around to the same way of thinking, so there is a move towards escalators that merely go slowly when no-one is near, and speed up when a *voyageur* steps on. This type is now being used in London, so there is a convergence of the systems.

Perhaps a better adjective for the Metro than 'small' is 'concentrated'. It has 225 route kilometres (140 miles) compared to the 400 kilometres (250 miles) of the London Underground, but then London is, as we have seen, fifteen times bigger than Paris proper, where most of that Metro kilometrage is located. Like Paris itself, it is high-density, and it actually has more stations than the Underground: 304 at the time of writing, compared to 272. A station seems to turn up whenever you want one, just as the trains do, and it was part of the original 1900 conception that every Parisian should live within 500 metres of a Metro station.

The Metro, then, serves Paris proper brilliantly, which

perhaps is a backhanded compliment, given the smallness of the city. It's as if Parisians are spoilt by their Metro, especially given how cheap it is: at the time of writing, a single journey is the equivalent of about £1.40, whereas a single journey between most London zones is more like £6 (or £4 with an Oyster card). The Metro could perhaps put its prices up, since it is the railway of the Metropolitan, and liberal, French elite – and perhaps the Metro contributes to that liberalism. In the *Financial Times* on 15 April 2022, the French journalist Agnès Poirier quoted some research that concluded, 'The further away people live from a railway station, the likelier they are to vote for Le Pen.' The *gilet-jaune* working-class protest movement – a 'crisis of failed urbanism', according to Paris's deputy mayor for urbanism, Jean-Louis Missika – was rooted in the suburbs, including those beyond Paris. The yellow vests are the kind worn by truckers. Roundabouts on busy roads became focal points of the campaign – so here were people without a Metro of their own. I happened to be in central Paris when one of those protests was underway, and a yellow-vested man who had apparently become detached from his fellow dissidents stared nastily at me as I crossed the boulevard St Michel. Perhaps he took me for a member of the Parisian elite ... or perhaps I flatter myself, because I have never achieved a Parisian sleekness.

In 2009, Richard Rogers was one of a number of architects invited to submit an architectural strategy to President Sarkozy for the Grand Paris project he had initiated. In the *Guardian* that year, Rogers was quoted as saying, 'I don't know any other major city where the heart is so much detached from its arms and legs,' and this tension between Paris and suburbs is central to the Metro story, as is the tension between Paris and France.

The term *banlieue*, meaning (ominously enough) 'banned from the place' has come to evoke low-cost housing, especially around the edge of Paris – *habitation à loyer modéré* (HLM) – that is in turn associated with social unrest. (Of course, there are posh Parisian suburbs, the most exclusive being Neuilly-sur-Seine, of which Sarkozy had been mayor, and which is served by the very clean and orderly Pont de Neuilly station – westerly terminus of Line 1 between 1937 and 1992 – but this is a '*banlieue aisée*' or comfortable suburb, a special case.)

Since medieval times, Paris has risen against the French state, and of course Paris was at the forefront of the 1789 insurrection. But if France feared Paris, the reverse was also true. 'Paris has been continually perceived as a threatened environment,' writes Norma Evenson in *Paris: A Century of Change 1878–1978*. And what exactly was under threat? Evenson quotes from *Studies of Paris* (1882) by the Italian novelist and poet Edmondo des Amicis, who wrote that 'the whole affair is different from that of London – the green open place, the faces, the voices, and the colours give to that confusion more the air of pleasure than of work ... Everything is open, transparent and places on view as at an elegant, great market in the open air.' But from the top of Notre Dame he saw 'away in the distance, on the horizon, across light violet mists ... uncertain outlines of smoking suburbs, behind which, nothing being visible, we still fancied Paris. On another side, other enormous suburbs, crowded upon the heights like armies ready to descend, full of sadness and menace.'

By the late twentieth century, the concentration of immigrants in the deprived *banlieues* had brought a racial element to this tension. In *Paris: The Secret History*, Andrew Hussey evokes the city in the aftermath of 9/11, when

> it became the craze for black and Arab youths from the poor parts of the city, or just beyond its periphery, to come into the shopping districts of the city centre – Les Halles, La Défense – to cause trouble. Dressed like black Americans, but with accents and manners from the Maghreb, these kids staged pitched battles, terrifying both shoppers and workers. Like the rhetorical violence in rap music – at which these Parisian suburbanites excel – the aim was to shock the jaded spectator into feeling something, anything.

On early Metro maps, Paris appeared as a blob full of Metro lines; the non-Metro railways and trams serving the suburbs were not shown. The Paris blob is a hard shape to describe; it's almost a pentagram tipped to the right, but I also think of it as a speech bubble arising from a mouth located in the south-west corner, somewhere near Porte de St Cloud. It seems a privileged territory. The first official Metro pocket map did not appear until 1912, and many of the early Metro maps were produced by upmarket shops, to show how you could access their premises. (Even today, the Metro map supplied to Eurostar passengers at St Pancras International has some crucial central detailing obliterated by an advert for Galeries Lafayette department store.) A map produced in 1914 by Le Bon Marché depicted bustling Paris in a creamy shade; the apparently deserted suburbs were beige. This use of colour to distinguish Paris from its hinterland – the place located *'extra muros'* or beyond the outer walls (which continued to exist notionally even after they were knocked down) – has continued today, although the transport possibilities of the suburbs are now indicated to a greater or lesser extent; at the very least, the Metro extensions into those suburbs, which began in the 1930s, are shown.

Early Metro maps, like the system itself, were often very attractive, with delicate pastels used for those distinguishing colours. But this prettiness seems disingenuous, a cover for the real message of the suburban colour: 'Here be monsters.' 'It is fascinating,' Mark Ovenden writes in *Paris Metro Style*, 'for non-Parisians to notice so many different makes of Metro maps (even to the present day) making such a concerted effort to show the walls or the shape of the city – almost as if acknowledging that there are some places outside the city walls which are so heinous they have to be locked out, or that Paris must constantly disassociate itself from the sprawl on its doorstep.'

I would urge the reader to keep in mind this tension between Paris and not-Paris, since it's a central theme of the chronology that follows, although not quite as important a theme, it seems to me, as the urge to make the Metro beautiful enough to be worthy of those privileged Parisians.

II

BEFORE THE METRO

A Problem of Circulation

In mid-nineteenth-century Paris, as in London, population was rising rapidly: from 786,000 in 1831 to over a million in 1848. In both cities there was a problem of circulation, fuelled by the increasing quantity of goods brought to the peripheries of the cities by main-line railways. From there, medieval forms of transport took over: that is, horses. Yes, in some cases this took the relatively progressive form of horse-drawn buses capable of carrying a couple of dozen people. Here, Paris had been ahead of London, and the pioneer – this being France – was a philosopher.

In 1662 Blaise Pascal obtained permission from Louis XIV to establish a network of timetabled carriages. His motivation was charitable: to raise funds for the poor of the Loire Valley and to improve the lives of the Parisian working class. But his coaches were commandeered by the wealthy and became symbols of privilege that were sometimes attacked and overturned by the underprivileged, just as Pascal's vision had been overturned.

French buses went dormant until the early nineteenth century when a M. Baudry started a service in Nantes. His depot was opposite a shop owned by a M. Omnes who advertised his

premises with the Latin slogan 'Omnes Omnibus', suggesting that he, Omnes, had something for everybody. The word
'omnibus' migrated to public carriages. In the 1820s Baudry
began operating a service in Paris, but he was overwhelmed
by competitors – a sign of the growing demand for mobility in
Paris; he went bankrupt and drowned himself in the Canal St
Martin in 1830.

The 'London bus' is really a French thing, in that George
Shillibeer, who introduced buses to London in the 1830s,
had started out by making buses for Paris. But buses were
not the answer, in Paris or London, and neither were horse-
drawn trams, which Paris also pioneered. They only added to
the traffic.

Paris needed not so much new vehicles as new streets. In
Paris: The Secret History, Andrew Hussey writes of 'an urban
infrastructure that had barely been touched or improved
since the late-medieval period'. 'There were no straight roads
through Paris,' he adds, 'whose centre, Île de la Cité, was a
dark and muddy labyrinth, rank with infection and crime'. The
problem of circulation was addressed between 1853 and 1870
by a man who would raze the fraught Île de la Cité as part of
his great rationalisation of Paris. Baron Haussmann, whose job
title was Prefect of the Seine – that is, the representative of the
state for the Paris *région* – was briefed by Napoleon III to *'aérer,
unifier et embellier'* Paris: to open up, unify, beautify.

Haussmann created a network of uniform boulevards (he
also formalised the woodlands to the west as the Bois de
Boulogne, those to the east as the Bois de Vincennes). At the

heart of the scheme was his *grande croisée*, where the boulevards
de Sebastopol and de Strasbourg intersected with the rue de
Rivoli at Châtelet. (The Metro would have its own *grande croisée*
when Lines 1 and 4 intersected at the same spot.) As part of
Haussmann's rationalisation, Paris was expanded, and this can
be understood in terms of the footprints of the Paris Walls.
The Grand or Interior Boulevards followed the walls built
by Charles V in the late fourteenth century and demolished
by Louis XIV in 1646. Immediately beyond these lay streets
occupying the territory bounded by the wall of the Farmers
General, not a defensive wall, but an eighteenth-century tax
barrier, whose course would be followed by the Circle-Line-
in-effect of the Paris Metro: Lines 2 and 6. This was the Paris
boundary until Haussmann appropriated the territory between
it and the furthest flung fortification: the Thiers Wall. By this,
the number of arrondissements was increased from twelve to
the present twenty. The suburbs thus appropriated had been
exempt from Paris taxes, and so had been the site of budding
industry, but they were now doomed to be beautified – the
chimneys torn down, furnaces extinguished. A kiss of death,
perhaps, but Paris didn't want such ugliness on its doorstep,
and the new territory would in due course be embraced by
the Metro.

Haussmann made Paris less cramped and insular; he opened
it up to France and – potentially – the French army. His radial
boulevards connected with the equally grand new railway stations, Gare du Nord and Gare de l'Est, and the rebuilt Gare de
Lyon, by which troops might enter the city to quell riots and

revolution – and there had been as many as six uprisings in Paris between 1830 and 1848. In practice there was only one post-Haussmann uprising: the Paris Commune of 1871, which sought to capitalise on the defeat of the French army in the Franco-Prussian War. The army re-took Paris, but by oblique manoeuvres, not by marching down the new boulevards. Nonetheless, the Parisian itch to lock the door against the state would inform its conception of the Metro.

For some commentators on Paris, including Richard Cobb, Haussmann denuded the city of all its character. For others, he made the city elegant and user-friendly, two qualities that would be shared by the Metro; but he did not solve the problem of circulation. In 1867, Paris hosted the International Exhibition: the first of three such events that would make Paris self-conscious about its inadequacies (just as any householder looks sceptically at their interior décor prior to giving a party), eventually prompting the building of the Metro. 'For all Haussmann's work, crowds of visitors had trouble getting around,' writes Benson Bobrick in *Labyrinths of Iron*, 'and the city was acutely embarrassed. Envy began to work on the French: across the Channel, as everyone knew, the arrogant English were going ahead with expansions of their Underground.'

London Decides: The Metropolitan Railway

In 1863, the Metropolitan Railway, the world's first urban underground railway, opened in London between

Paddington – on the fringes of countryside to the west – and
Farringdon, on the edge of the so-called City of London: a distance of 8 miles. At the time, the square mile of the City was a
district of small workshops, and it had the densest residential
population of anywhere in London; today, as the financial district, it is the least densely populated. In 1863, the fringes of
the City were also counted as rookeries, or slums.

One aim of the Metropolitan Railway was to reduce traffic
congestion. In the 1840s there was talk of the 'omnibus nuisance' in central London. There was also a hackney carriage
nuisance, a private carriage nuisance, a cart-and-wagon nuisance and a horse-and-rider nuisance. In *The History of the
London Underground Map*, Caroline Roope describes how the
main-line railways, newly arrived on the edges of the capital,
made the traffic 'locks' or 'blocks' worse:

> These stations had been built on outlying land that could
> be purchased cheaply, such as London Bridge (1836), mean-
> ing that travellers to the city would have to complete their
> journey by road. This added further congestion to the
> streets – some of which were not fit for purpose, having
> been built in the Middle Ages, long before omnibuses and
> carriages were in use.

But the Metropolitan Railway had a nobler purpose than
merely reducing congestion. Charles Pearson, the man behind
the Met, was an altruist, who had campaigned for the right of
Jews to hold public office, and against capital punishment. Like

Blaise Pascal, he was a *transportation* altruist, but he was more worldly than Pascal. Pearson was a lawyer – solicitor to the Corporation of London (the body that ran the City) – and he saw the good that trains could do, whereas many people saw only the bad. To Charles Dickens, who was nostalgically fond of stagecoaches, trains were despoilers of the countryside and the bringers of deadening corporate uniformity, by which the country was ruled by a single, sinister clock ('It was as if the sun itself had given in,' he writes in *Dombey and Son*). They were also murderous. Trains kill people in *Dombey* and in Dickens's famous short story, 'The Signalman', written shortly after the railways had done their best to kill Dickens himself. Returning on a boat train from Northern France with his mistress, Ellen Ternan, in 1865, he was involved in the Staplehurst train crash, in which ten people died.

Dickens's critique of railways was widespread among land-owners, who didn't want trains rushing through their fields, until they saw how much money they could extract from them. The middle classes also softened towards railways when they realised they could bring them a country home to go with their city job. In the 1840s, the city merchants were beginning to move out to the burgeoning suburbs – those places now considered part of central London, like Camberwell, Islington, Hackney. They might make the journey by private carriage or horse-drawn omnibus, but increasing numbers were travelling in and out of 'town' by train.

Charles Pearson called this diurnal movement 'oscillation', whereas we would say 'commuting', an American term that didn't cross the Atlantic until the early twentieth century and never made it to France. Pearson didn't see why the working classes shouldn't oscillate. In his railway vision, the people of the City rookeries would live in villages north of London, travelling every morning on trains drawn by atmospheric power, so as to be smokeless (Pearson reckoned the working classes had had enough of smoke), to a great half-underground complex with thirty platforms beneath the City streets. 'Pearson's vision to alleviate congestion wasn't the real driving force of his proposal,' writes Caroline Roope in *The History of the London Underground Map*. 'At the heart of his campaigning lay a genuine desire to improve the dismal and squalid conditions in which the poor and slum-dwelling classes routinely lived. This he hoped could be achieved by housing workers in the less-polluted suburban districts ... away from the ills of the metropolis.'

In 1846, Charles Pearson told a Royal Commission on Metropolitan Termini: 'The passion for a country residence is increasing to an extent that it would be impossible to persons who do not mix much with the poor to know. You cannot find a place where they do not get a broken teapot in which to stuff, as soon as spring comes, some flower or something to give them an idea of green fields and the country.'

A flower might as well have been adopted as the symbol of what became London Underground, because its primary purpose was to take people *out* of London. Within thirty years of its inauguration, the Metropolitan Railway would boast a country branch terminating 24 miles out of central London.

The Paris Metro, by contrast, lived up to its name. It would mainly be concerned with increasing circulation and reducing congestion in Paris proper. The Metro wouldn't grope its way into the suburbs until the 1930s; it would be insular, the Underground outgoing.

The Metropolitan Railway became a reality when Pearson's scheme was adapted to lure investment. Instead of going north from London, it would run west, connecting the City with the countryside in that direction, but also with Paddington Station, headquarters of the Great Western Railway, which sought a connection to the City. The Great Western invested in the Met, which, at King's Cross, provided a connection for a second main-line: the Great Northern. Later, the Midland Railway would also be connected to the Met. There was a continuum between the Met and the national network. The opposite situation would obtain in Paris, where the Metro would shun the main-lines.

The Metropolitan Railway might be thought of as providing a feeder line into central London for those main-lines, but that's not quite correct. It provided a feeder to the edge of the square mile of the City, which lies east of Westminster, usually considered the heart of London. That Royal Commission of 1846 had recommended against the building of railway stations of any kind in central London, the aim being to protect the rights of West End landlords such as the Earl of Cadogan and the Duke of Westminster. The ban of 1846 was not observed absolutely, and it melted away with the coming of Tube railways – that is, deep-level lines – to the Underground, which began in 1890, with the opening of the City and South London Railway. The Tubes were sufficiently deep to leave the basements of West End mansions undisturbed.

Once the 1846 ban had faded away, London and its suburbs became a continuum: there is a difference between the London postal district and the wider concept of Greater London, but most people can't say what it is, and it doesn't really matter, whereas every Parisian knows exactly where Paris ends. London became ever 'greater' because the London Underground kept expanding, and house builders followed the railway lines. The expansion of the Underground took place in a series of leaps during the inter-war period, with the opening of long line extensions rather than just a few new outlying stations at a time in the Parisian manner. The expansion was promoted by governments as a means of stimulating the economy in the Depression, and it made London into a commuter city. The stereotypical late Victorian commuter was Mr Pooter, depicted by George and Weedon Grossmith in their comic novel of 1893, *The Diary of a Nobody*. Mr Pooter *is* the nobody. He commutes by bus from the new suburb of Holloway – which today would be considered as more or less central London – to the City: a distance of about 4 miles. But the commutes would become longer.

Paradoxically, a kind of snobbery drove aspirational Londoners further and further out. 'During the nineteenth century', writes Simon Webb in *Commuters: The History of a British Way Of Life*, 'the middle classes moved to smart suburbs and then abandoned them and moved further outwards as the areas where they lived became less desirable; which is to say, more working-class. The consequence was that the further away from the city centre one moved, the smarter and more expensive became the district. The most posh suburbs always tended to be those on the outer extremity of cities; next to the open country.'

Insofar as there was tension between inhabitants of central London and suburbanites, it took the form of gentle satire, poking fun at the staidness of the commuter, his enthrallment to his job and his routine. John Betjeman specialised in this genre. In 1973, he wrote and presented his celebrated documentary, *Metroland*, taking the mickey out of the suburbia created by the Metropolitan Railway. In Neasden, he meets Mr Eric Simms, birdwatcher, who's proud of discovering *rus in urbe*: 'Altogether I've seen ninety species of bird within half an hour of my home, and I must say that's not at all bad.' At the end of the film, Betjeman comes to the end of the line: 'The houses of Metroland never got as far as Verney Junction. Grass triumphs. And I must say I'm rather glad.' In 1961, Tony Hancock had starred as Tony, a frustrated commuter, in *The Rebel*, scripted by himself, with Ray Galton and Alan Simpson. 'Journey number six thousand, eight hundred and eighty-three,' he sighs, as he settles into the morning train, dark-suited and bowler-hatted like everyone else in the carriage. The satirists were aided by the fact that British commuters wore a uniform. Tony aspires to be an artist. As he explains to his landlady, he paints in the Impressionist style. 'Well, it doesn't impress me at all,' she replies.

To escape the commuting life (and pursue his artistic calling),

Tony moves to Paris, which seems symbolically significant. In Paris, the commuter is not a stock figure of fun. He or she might be considered a threat. In France, the word for commuter is, or can be, *banlieusard*, and the term *banlieue*, meaning suburb, is loaded, carrying the implication of 'outsider'. Certainly, the *banlieusards* of Paris would be outside the reach of the Metro for many years.

Paris Dithers, Then Decides

'In 1882', writes Clive Lamming in *The Story of the Paris Metro*, 'City of Paris officials discovered that vehicle traffic at the intersection of the boulevard Montmartre and rue Montmartre (nicknamed "the crossroads of the crushed") numbered more than 100,000 per day!' Action was required, but in 1882 Paris had been agonising over the form its own metro might take for seventeen years, and it would continue to do so until 1898.

The opening of the Metropolitan in London triggered contempt, jealousy, a desire to go one better – and inertia. Paris didn't exactly know how to go one better, and it wasn't necessarily a free agent, because the national government would want a say. What did seem clear was that Paris wouldn't go down the steam train route for its metro. Clive Lamming writes that Paris, 'City of Light, capital of good taste and reason', would be unlikely to build a railway that smoked its passengers 'like kippers', and in the last decade of the nineteenth century electric trains would begin to look increasingly viable.

The Metropolitan was a railway ahead of its time with trains that were *of* its time: steam trains, and even though the engines were fitted with condensing gear that was supposed to retain the steam and smoke, in practice the drivers released it, because the engines were more efficient if the mechanism could breathe. The platforms were lit by gas lights in glass globes that swung in the breeze from an arriving train, and the gas burned yellow from all the impurities in the air. The drivers of the engines grew beards to try to filter the smoke and steam. The Met knew it had an air-quality problem, hence the ban on smoking imposed from the outset. (In 1874 the ban was overturned on civil liberties grounds.) Trains were shortened to reduce the stress on the engines and therefore, supposedly, emissions. But in his novel of 1887, *In the Year of Jubilee*, George Gissing places two of his characters on the Met at King's Cross, noting: 'They stood together on the platform, among hurrying crowds, in black fumes that poisoned the palate with sulphur.'

It's surprising, given the negative publicity surrounding the Metropolitan Railway, that Paris should adopt its name, but the evolving plans for an urban railway in the city would be known as *'réseau metropolitain'* or 'metropolitan network', and this was popularly abbreviated to 'Metro', whereas when 'Metropolitan Railway' was abbreviated in London, it was to 'Met', which suits the London accent better than 'Metro'. And the Paris abbreviation caught on in much of the rest of the world, from Moscow to Mexico City.

*

In 1865, the French government gave local authorities power to build railways '*d'intérêt local*' (of local importance), the sort of grudging concession that characterises a centralised state. In 1872, the city council produced a plan for a local underground railway – two intersecting lines following the *grand croisée* of Paris and surrounded by a circle. The plan proved abortive. In 1875, the Prefect of the Seine (the state representative) proposed a central underground station beneath the Palais Royal. Its lines would radiate out to the main-line termini, so this would not be a local plan but a national one, to be built by the state. The city council objected that this would not serve the needs of Parisians, whereas the central government wanted any Parisian railway to be integrated into the national network just as the Metropolitan in London gave access to the Great Western and the Great Northern. The involvement of the main-lines in the Metropolitan Railway was purely commercial, whereas the French government was, as Brian Hardy writes in *Paris Metro Handbook*, 'mindful of strategic use in time of civil or external war', both of which had occurred in 1870–71. These were the battle lines of a stand-off that would continue for a quarter of a century, during which time many plans for Parisian railways came and, mostly, went.

The plans were very disparate. Some reached out into the suburbs, following Pearson's idea for London: allow the poor to find better, and cheaper, housing on the fringes of the country-side. This was resisted by those who thought Paris would thus be depopulated, that 'grass would grow in certain quarters,' as Olivier de Landreville wrote in *Les Grands Travaux de Paris*

(1887). Most of the schemes focused on the city proper. Some plans were for elevated railways, even though the New York elevated railways of the 1870s (four lines running down four avenues), precursors of the New York Subway, had received a bad press. A network of viaducts would create shadows in the 'city of light'.

On the other hand, there was a persistent idea that Parisians were too noble to travel underground, and in 1878 Louis Heuzé, an architect who had proposed an elevated railway, said that any subterranean one would be a 'Nécropolitain', therefore shunned by the citizenry. In 1884, Jules Garnier, another advocate of elevation, wrote, in a document called *Avant Projet d'Un Chemin de Fer Aérien*: 'What difference does it make to an inhabitant of London if he is surrounded by vapour, darkness and smoke; he is in the same condition above ground. But take the Parisian who loves the day, the sun, gaiety and colour around him, and propose that he alter his route to seek, in darkness, a means of transport which will be a foretaste of the tomb, and he will refuse, preferring the *impériale* of an omnibus.' (*'Impériale'* being the poetic name for the upper decks, of which there are none left on Paris municipal buses.)

But Parisians had already been given a foretaste of the tomb. The Paris Catacombs, by the way, are an ossuary containing the remains of several million Parisians, transferred in the late eighteenth century from overflowing cemeteries in central Paris. The Catacombs occupy a tunnel that had once served the Paris quarries, which is located (rather tactlessly) just south of the Barrière d'Enfer, 'Gate of Hell', a tollhouse in the Wall of

the Farmers General. In the realm of death, as in public transport, Paris resisted the ranginess of London. When London
graveyards were overflowing in the mid-nineteenth century, a
great cemetery was created 30 miles to the south, at Brookwood
in Surrey, with a special railway to serve it. This was London's
notion of 'extra-mural interment'. Paris, by contrast, removed
its bodies just a short distance beyond the city wall. Today, the
Catacombs are a tourist attraction, and the nearest station is
Denfert-Rochereau on Metro Lines 4 and 6. Denfert-Rochereau
is named after Place Denfert-Rochereau, which is in turn
named after General Pierre Denfert-Rochereau, who led the
resistance to the Prussian siege of the city of Belfort in the
Franco-Prussian War. I wonder whether the same subcon-
scious allurement that drew the ossuary to the Gate of Hell
was involved here too, since 'Denfert' is pronounced in French
in the same way as 'd'Enfer'.

In 1881, Jean Chrétien had proposed an electric 'el', running
along the major boulevards on 6-metre-high viaducts. It would
cross in front of the Opéra, and Chrétien anticipated the con-
cerns here in a document of 1881, *Chemin de Fer Électrique de
Boulevards à Paris*. He starts out conciliatory: 'It is possible …
to give this part of the projected work a character either monumental or decorative, which would render it worthy to be
placed on this spot without disfiguring it.' He then becomes
slightly provocative, suggesting 'many believe that the Place
de l'Opéra would gain by being a bit more furnished than it is'.
Finally, he is outright rude, contending that a metro will be
more useful than the Opéra, which costs 'four to five million

a year, for a questionable result'. When a Ligue Parisienne du Metropolitain Aérien was founded in 1887, a counter group was formed, the Société des Amis des Monuments Parisiens, and Charles Garnier, designer of the Opéra (as opposed to Jules Garnier the 'el' advocate), was president of it.

By this time, Paris had seen schemes for elevated railways on monorails, on the riverbanks, or running along the centre of the river itself. These were all designed to spare the boulevards, but another scheme of the 1880s, put forward by the engineers Dupuis, Vibart and Varrailhon, proposed a metal viaduct cutting through boulevards and actual buildings at right angles. This would require the demolition of only part of any building, the trio contended; the rest would remain habitable – so people might find themselves living in an apartment with a Metro line as next-door neighbour. A scheme pushed by the engineer Arsène-Olivier envisaged viaducts 30 metres high that would clear the roofs of most buildings. *Voyageurs* would ascend to the tracks using lifts in the buildings below.

There were also the underground men. One scheme envisaged trains running underground gravitationally on descending gradients, before being hoisted by lifts for another descent. There was a scheme to build a network of tunnels that would be a railway by day, a sewer by night. Ventilators and fans would clear the smell every morning. A plausible subterranean scheme was put forward by Jean Baptiste Berlier in 1887. His plan was for an east–west deep-level railway – 'abundantly ventilated and luxuriously illuminated' – of metal tubes through which electric trains would run: in other words, a tube line of the kind that would open in London in 1890 in the form of the City & South London Railway, which put further pressure on Paris to get a move on.

In 1892, the city council approved Berlier's scheme – envisaged as running from Porte de Vincennes to Porte Dauphine, roughly the route of what eventually became Line 1 of the Metro – with no resistance from central government. Berlier could not raise the funds for construction, so the project lapsed; but we have not heard the last of the visionary and aesthetic Berlier. In May 1896, the pressure increased when the first underground railway in continental Europe was opened in Budapest: an electric railway using overhead power transmission. (All the charm of the Budapest Metro is concentrated in Line 1, which is the oldest of the three on the network, being the ground-breaking line of 1896. The stations are white-tiled as on the Paris Metro, but boxy and small. Each contains a wooden booth for the sale of tickets. These booths were all closed when I last visited Budapest, but endearingly so, with purple velvet curtains drawn across the ticket windows. As for the trains, they were like small yellow trams that made electrical fizzing noises as they stopped and started.)

In *The Story of the Paris Metro*, Clive Lamming writes that 'feelings of jealousy and shame' triggered in Paris by the Budapest opening were magnified when the Glasgow Subway opened in December 1896, Glasgow being regarded in France as 'a relatively sleepy damp town engulfed in mist'.

*

Worsening traffic congestion and the approach of the Universal Exposition of 1900 forced the issue. Parisian transport had proved inadequate during the two previous Expositions, in 1867 and 1889. (Paris was the exposition city: there would be eight of them between 1855 and 1937.) Now the city had to live up to its new century. Paris, the beautiful woman, was hosting a very grand party, and she must decide what to wear. In 1895, Louis Barthou, the Minister of the Interior, granted Paris the power to create and control the new railway, and a law of 30 March 1898 formalised a plan for six electrified lines: two running west to east (Lines 1 and 3); two running north–south (Lines 4 and 5), and a circular route (2 and 6). In other words, a cross in a circle. This plan was approved by law the following year. A plan for more lines – an 'additional network' of the Metro – would be agreed in 1907.

But the city remained wary of the state. Paris's first intention was to keep out the main-lines by building the Metro to a track gauge narrower than the national one, but the government insisted on standard-gauge track as a condition of approval. The city then implemented its Plan B without consulting the government: it made the loading gauge of the Metro trains (that is, their dimensions) smaller than that of the national network trains. Metro trains are about 2.5m wide, whereas the national trains were about 3.20. The Metro tunnels were thus too small for national trains. So Paris was behaving like a disaffected lover who changes the locks to keep out their 'ex'.

III

A BRIEF CHRONOLOGY
OF THE METRO

The Neatness of Bienvenüe

Six companies bid for the Metro concession; the winner was the Compagnie Général de Traction, backed by the flamboyant Belgian financier, Édouard Empain (Baron Empain), who built trams and railways around the world. We should not be surprised at some of the exotic aspects of the Metro, given that Empain was an Egyptologist whose Heliopolis Oasis Company created Heliopolis, an affluent suburb of Cairo, where he lived in a mansion built in Hindu style. For the purpose of building the Metro, the Compagnie Général de Traction renamed itself Compagnie du Chemin de Fer Metropolitain de Paris (CMP). The Paris Council would build the infrastructure: tunnels, viaducts, stations. The CMP would supply the superstructure – tracks, signals, station entrances – and operate the trains. The CMP's concession would last twenty-five years, during which the city would receive a portion of the fares collected.

This strong municipal direction is often contrasted with the laissez-faire approach (it's paradoxical that the term is French) taken to the building of the London Underground and railways generally in Britain. But in *Cities, Railways, Modernities* (2019), Carlos López Galviz questions the idea of 'Paris as one of the most iconic models of modern town planning and of London as a result of piecemeal visions, chance and patchwork'. The true picture, he writes, 'is more nuanced'. Governmental decree kept the early cut-and-cover lines out of the middle of London, for instance, and required the Metropolitan and District railways to work together to build the Circle Line (which they did with the greatest ill grace). The planning of the Metro was not perfect, and the system today shows evidence of some confusion about how it should evolve, but it certainly got off to a good start. Construction began in November 1898, and Line 1 opened in July 1900, to immediate acclaim – and the *voyageurs* flocked to it and the subsequent lines. The whole of that first Metro network scheme would be completed by January 1910, a year ahead of schedule, at which point we invite the Chief Engineer to step forward and take a bow.

Fulgence Bienvenüe first made his mark on Paris as an engineer for the city working in two of its poorest, and hilliest, arrondissements, the 19th and the 20th. In the 1880s, he built the Belleville funicular cable railway; he is also reputed to have assisted in the development of Buttes-Chaumont Park, which is railway-haunted, as we will be seeing.

He was born in 1852 in the northern coastal village of Uzel in Brittany, the thirteenth child of a lawyer. A dapper, slight man whose straight nose and very horizontal moustache formed a *grande croisée* of their own, he was even slighter than nature intended, because, as a young engineer, he'd lost his left arm in a railway accident. He had been presenting a newly built railway in Mayenne, north-west France, to a *jury d'expropriation*, a government committee that decided on public investments.

When he told the story in later life, he liked to say, 'I was expropriated from my left arm,' which reflects the genuine sang-froid of his character. After the accident, he tended to be photographed from the right, to hide his disability, but a picture of him dating from the 1930s (if his stylish fedora is anything to go by) was taken from the left. He stands at the entrance to Monceau station on Line 6, and perhaps that station's beautiful Guimard entrance emboldened him to face the camera in that way. The wagon that ran him over was an escapee from a steam train, so you can see why he favoured electricity for the Metro. 'By the enchanted lightning of Jupiter', Bienvenüe declared, 'the race of Prometheus is transported to the depths,' only he said it in Latin, being an enthusiastic classicist. He was a romantic as well as a classicist, however, and he favoured candlelight in his own home. This duality would occur on his Metro: severe modernity down below, yet the whimsicality of the Guimard entrances above.

Bienvenüe projected his own neatness and elegance onto the Metro. He used what was called the 'Belgian method' for most of his excavations, by which the crown of the tunnel is created first, so the road could be quickly restored while the lower part of the tunnel was excavated below. And he was committed to clearing up as soon as possible the disruption the digging would cause. (There's a famous shot of the rue Rivoli transformed into an enormous hole in front of the Hôtel de Ville; even the workmen look stunned.)

The lines would be independent of one another, to avoid complicated junctions at which trains would have to wait for another to pass, as they do on the London Underground. There would be no flat crossings. Where lines did cross, it was by flying junctions, one going over the other. All trains would run to the end of the line calling at all stations. In the early days of electric traction, there was a single discrete locomotive or power car at the front, and this always had to remain at the front, since it was where the driver sat. At the ends of the lines, this power car could be returned to the front by 'running around' its carriages: that is, being detached, running onto a siding, and moving to the new front end. But Bienvenüe preferred the less fussy method of having the trains – and sometimes also the passengers – run around a loop at the line ends. We will be returning to the Metro loops.

This simple end-to-end operating meant that when a train called at a station, everyone waiting on the platform would know where it was going. Compare the situation in London, where everyone waiting for a northbound train on the West End branch of the Northern Line must check whether it's destined for Edgware or High Barnet (or indeed Golders Green or Mill Hill East), and perhaps they forget to check, in which case there's a good chance they will board the wrong train. And there would be no skipping of stops by express trains on the Metro, as happens on the New York Subway and occasionally on the Underground. As things turned out, there would be a couple of junctions on the Metro to complicate matters, but they went against the grain with Bienvenüe.

Fulgence Bienvenüe became synonymous with the Metro. His very first name suggests lightning or by implication electricity, and but for the diaresis over the 'u' his surname would mean 'Welcome', which seems fitting, given the man's public-spiritedness. In 1933, Avenue du Maine station, then serving Line 5, was renamed in his honour, and shortly before the ceremony, it was realised that the diaresis over the 'u' had been left off the station signs. It was hastily added. This station was linked to Montparnasse Station in 1942, so it is now Montparnasse-Bienvenüe, but many *voyageurs*, even French ones, apparently, take the name to mean 'Montparnasse-Welcome'. In this way, Bienvenüe seems to have magnanimously disappeared into the network he created.

Bienvenüe is known as the 'father of the Metro'. There is no equivalent for the London Underground, which reflects its multi-various, free-market origins – unless we count Charles Yerkes, but he died before the lines he inaugurated were opened, whereas Bienvenüe would continue as Chief Engineer of the Metro until he retired in 1932, aged eighty. He died in 1936, and one summer's afternoon of broiling heat I attempted to find his grave in Père Lachaise cemetery. As you emerge from the station named after the cemetery, the exuberant Guimard entrance looks irreverent, being so close to all that Gothic gloom. In the cemetery, signs direct the visitor to the approximate locations of the famous dead, but after an hour of searching, the dazzling sunlight refracting off the pale stone of the tombs (the chestnut trees of the cemetery shade the walkways for the living rather than the graves of the dead) and the smell of flowers decaying in the heat were giving me a migraine. I was on the point of giving up when I found the last resting place of M. Bienvenüe. On the grave is a sculpted palm; half a dozen warped Metro tickets had been jammed into the stone fronds.

Crossing the Border

Most of the early Metro was operated by the CMP, which was a private company, but working under the close supervision of the Paris Council, which had built the infrastructure. There was also some private sector involvement, in that the Société du Chemin de Fer Électrique Souterrain Nord-Sud de Paris – the Nord-Sud – built and operated its own two Metro lines, opened in 1910 and 1911. The Nord-Sud was the creation of the same Jean-Baptiste Berlier who had proposed a 'tubular underground tramway' for Paris, and who had experience of sending things through Tubes, since he'd developed Paris's pneumatic postal system. The original plan of the Nord-Sud was also to build deep-level, tube-like lines, so escaping the need to follow the boulevards (which the Metro generally does), but tube railways are expensive to create, so the Nord-Sud lines would be close to the surface and built by cut-and-cover like those of the CMP. The Paris Council took a cut of Nord-Sud ticket revenue, just as it did from the CMP, and in 1930 the latter would absorb the former.

In its first thirty years, the Metro was a municipal railway, operated by and for the city of Paris. Here is Alon Levy, from an article entitled 'The French Way of Building Rapid Transit', posted in June 2020 on his Pedestrian Observations website: 'The Metro was a municipal effort run by the municipal CMP, designed around the city's needs, which included not just good transportation but also separation from the working-class suburbs.'

But the population of the suburbs was rising rapidly; their transport needs had to be served. In 1929, an agreement was reached between the Paris Council, the CMP and the Department of the Seine (an administrative unit comprising Paris and its immediate suburbs, with governmental oversight in the person of the Prefect), by which the CMP was given a financial incentive to push out into the suburbs. These extensions we can imagine having been drafted by a small flick of a sharp pencil, whereas the London Underground extensions were drafted by somebody taking a dirty great crayon (a black or blue one in the case of the Northern and Piccadilly Line extensions of the 1920s and Thirties) and drawing a long line with a ruler. The Underground extensions usually went out to open fields, a lure to housebuilders, and where the Underground initiated suburb-building, the Metro followed it, and the extensions were done on a case-by-case basis: to serve a new housing development, factory, bus station. The first 'cross-border' extension of the Metro proper came in early 1934, when Line 9 was extended from Porte de Saint Cloud to Pont de Sèvres to the west of Paris.

Three years later, the CMP made a statement of suburban intent when it took over the Ligne de Sceaux that ran south for 10 kilometres from a station at Denfert-Rochereau in south

Paris, mainly through fields, to the strangely named (if you're English) village of Sceaux, where Parisians liked to go for a Sunday stroll and donkey rides.

In the 1860s the line, which had been opened in the 1840s with a broad-gauge track and experimental trains that could negotiate its tight curves, was extended beyond Sceaux. In the 1890s it was converted to standard gauge and its north end was extended further into central Paris, progressing first to a pretty pavilion-like station, Port-Royal, then on to a new underground terminus, Gare du Luxembourg. So here was this yokel line plodding right up to the gilded gates of the Jardin du Luxembourg, a strange meeting of country railway with a sophisticated pastiche of countryside. In the 1920s and 1930s, the countryside between Paris and Sceaux succumbed to the building of cheap houses, hence the interest of the CMP in what was now, in effect, a commuter line.

The CMP electrified the line (overhead) along some of its length, supplied it with trains resembling squat Spragues (the dauntingly named Z-stock) and treated it as an honorary Metro line, a sort of country cousin. It wasn't given a number like the other Metro lines, but it did appear on the Metro map, designated by an 'S'. Substations along the line bore signs reading 'Metropolitain', and in the 1970s its actual stations were awarded the yellow 'M' Metro totems.

Ian Nairn evoked Place Denfert-Rochereau in *Nairn's Paris* (1968). 'A number of random objects make it go,' he wrote. 'Item: one replica Lion de Belfort, one Metro, one station on the mysterious Ligne de Sceaux, a short stretch of the *ligne* itself uncovered just below the surface, several stalls, one impeccably legal gambling station, one Wallace fountain, one pissoir and one w.c. . . .' (Nairn's predilections were no secret: in his Preface to *Nairn's Paris*, he describes himself as 'a person who drinks a lot', and I wonder which of the several bustling bars at Place Denfert-Rochereau he observed it from.)

Today, the former Ligne de Sceaux station at Place Denfert-Rochereau is less 'mysterious', because in 1977 the line came into its own – or you could say lost its identity – as the southern prong of RER Line B. The line as it was in the 1950s is shown in the harrowing climactic scenes of the classic heist film *Rififi* (released in 1955), and the slovenly drug dealer, who rides the train out to its terminus at Saint-Rémy-lès-Chevreuse, refers to the line as 'the Metro'. Compelling as those scenes are in terms of the film's plot, I was annoyed not to be able to see the colour of the Z-stock trains, the film being in black and white. But Brian Patton and his *Paris RER Handbook* came to my aid. 'The Z stock was originally painted duck-egg blue, with a white roof,' he writes, 'the doors and windows of the first-class section being outlined in red. The roofs were painted dark grey during the war, and this attractive but slightly impractical livery gave way after 1946 to standard dreary SNCF green with black roof.'

The War and Its Effects

In 1938 French main-line railways were nationalised as SNCF, the Société Nationale des Chemins de Fer Francais.

Immediately after the Occupation of Paris in June 1940, almost half the Metro stations were closed, and such trains as did run were half-empty. Services were gradually restored, but Lines 2 and 6 remained closed because of the vulnerability to bombing of their elevated sections.

In 1943, there was then a sudden leap: the Metro carried 1.32 billion passengers, compared to 761 million in 1938. One factor was that petrol supply was severely limited, so few cars took to the roads. Supplies of heating fuel were also restricted, and the Metro offered warmth, light – and escape, in that it could take people to bars, restaurants, theatres, cinemas, many of which had been shut in 1942. But everything was constrained by curfews, as if Paris were a city of children who must go early to bed, and it was necessary to catch 'the last Metro' home at the end of the evening. The last trains ran at quarter to twelve (as opposed to 1 a.m. in normal times), and anyone wandering the streets after then was liable to be arrested and held as a hostage, or bargaining counter, by the German occupier, and acts of resistance could result in execution.

In London, missing the last train is the stuff of knockabout comedy; not in wartime Paris. In *The Story of the Paris Metro,* Clive Lamming writes that the phrase 'last Metro' became a 'cultural icon'. It was also the title of a film of 1980 by François Truffaut, concerning members of a theatre company who are resisting the Occupation in diverse ways. The title seems to be metaphorical, because we don't see anyone either catching or missing the last train, and the Metro makes only one appearance, in a brief clip of what looks like black and white archive footage, which makes a dream-like contrast to the vivid colour of the rest of the film, as if footage from a different film has been accidentally cut in. Perhaps Truffaut wanted to interpolate an image of a lost, civilised normality, to show what was being fought over.

From June 1942 all Jews in the occupied zone had to wear a yellow Star of David bearing the word *'Juif'*, and they were required to ride in the last carriage of Metro trains, which became known as 'synagogues'. In *Resistance: The French Fight Against the Nazis*, Matthew Cobb writes that Parisians seemed 'to have gone out of their way to express their solidarity with the Jews, and some young people even wore yellow stars with their own slogans ("Breton", "Aryan", "Honorary Jew")'. He quotes Hélène Barr, a twenty-one-year-old Jewish Parisienne who in July 1942 wrote in her diary: 'And then there's the sympathy of the people in the street, on the Metro. Men and women look at you with such goodness that it fills your heart with inexpressible feeling.'

The CMP couldn't survive the war. 'The Paris Metro company ... had slavishly ensured that collaboration in the capital went smoothly,' writes Matthew Cobb in *Eleven Days in August: The Liberation of Paris in 1944*,

creating a dedicated police service in the Metro to stop people defacing German posters, and setting aside vehicles for use by the German troops in the period following D-Day. Following a proposal by Léo Hamon at one of the last meetings of the CPL [the Comité Parisien de la Libération], the Metro company was taken under state control, although the wealthy shareholders, who had happily trousered the profits from the company's collaborationist activities, were all generously compensated.

The CMP was absorbed into the state-owned Régie Autonome des Transports Parisiens (RATP) in 1949.

We have seen that in 1929 the remit of the CMP had been expanded beyond Paris, and the RATP would also be required to serve the suburbs as well as the city. The definition of what is called, sometimes loosely, 'the Paris area' or 'Paris region' or (even more loosely) the 'Paris agglomeration' has evolved confusingly, but we are on solid ground from 1976, with the emergence of the Île de France, which is one of eighteen French *régions*, and comprises the Department of Paris and seven other *départements*. The RATP serves this area and operates the Paris buses and trams as well as the Metro. The city, incidentally, repented of its abolition of trams in 1938 (as in London, it had been thought they were getting in the way of cars), and they were re-introduced beyond the city borders in the early 1990s.

Immediately after the war, Parisians shunned the Metro, resenting having been forced on to it by wartime exigencies. 'In 1950 the Metro was deserted,' writes Clive Lamming in *The Story of the Paris Metro*, 'but the roadways were clogged.' Parisians were 'charmed' by their Renault 4CVs or 'the nippy Citroën 2CV'.

In the 1950s, the RATP budget was tightly restricted by French governments, and the main development of that decade was not Metro expansion but something more modest, albeit ingenious: the development of rubber-tyred trains, which were intended for all Metro lines until the project proved too expensive (since the track must be adapted to receive the trains), so only five lines would receive them. Tyres permit faster acceleration and braking than solid metal wheels. Tyre-shod trains are also quieter – and they do whisk rather than clatter in and out of stations. Another consideration was probably that they reminded people of cars at a time when cars were seen as glamorous and whose ownership was booming,.

Nevertheless, the Metro was suddenly in danger of looking outmoded.

Paris Turned Inside Out

The automobile achieved its Parisian apotheosis with the construction, between 1958 and 1973, of the orbital motorway, the Boulevard Périphérique. Richard Cobb wrote that the Périphérique 'circles Paris with the constant roar of tyres, the screams of sirens and the presence of sudden death'. For him, the road was one of the 'follies' of post-war Paris. He made these observations in a review of Norma Evenson's *Paris: A Century of Change (1878–1978)* that appears in a collection of his writings called *Paris and Elsewhere*, and in which he speaks of the 'schemes for the assassination of Paris' dreamed up between 1900 and the 1960s. (*The Assassination of Paris* was the title of a polemical book by Louis Chevalier much admired by Cobb.)

Many such plans, Cobb wrote, reflected 'a false priority, an obsession with the improvement of internal circulation ... Paris for the automobile, rather than Paris for the Parisians.' To Cobb's mind, the modernist architect le Corbusier was particularly murderous: 'Here he is already in 1925 obsessed with his own *grande croisée*, a swath of huge expressways cutting through the centre of Paris like a hot-cross bun.' Other 'horrors' were realised: Montparnasse Tower 'sticks up like a threat from another planet', and Tour Zamansky 'dwarfs the beautiful proportions of the tip of the Île Saint-Louis'.

'Paris doit épouser son siècle' ('Paris will marry its century'), wrote Paul Delouvrier, Prefect of the Seine, in 1963. Despite owning a particularly beautiful and historic house on that same Île Saint-Louis, President Pompidou agreed, so an expressway was created along the Right Bank of the Seine (it is currently pedestrianised), and it was Pompidou who presided at the opening of the Périphérique.

Richard Cobb writes that Pompidou got his *'trou'*, his hole (his excavation or building site), in the form of the Pompidou Centre, which Cobb compares to 'a gigantic *paupiette de veau* with all its innards displayed on the outside'. This was the centrepiece of the redevelopment of the Marais, formerly an area of small manufacturers, now a chic upper-middle-class quarter. Its working-class residents were shunted to the suburbs, and Cobb laments above all 'the de-Parisianisation of Paris': the removal from the city of much of its traditional population. He dates this from 1919, a result of the introduction of the eight-hour day and the development of the suburban railway network (big trains, not the Metro). Former Parisians were housed in outlying *'cités jardins'*, which gave way to the HBM blocks (*habitations à bon marché* – literally, cheap housing) of the interwar years, fore-runners of the *habitations à loyer modéré* (HLM) of the 1970s.

In 1901, the population of Paris was 2,700,000; that of the suburbs 955,000; in 1931 the figures were 2,900,000 and 2,100,000. There were still cheap places to live in Paris, such as *meublés*: rentable furnished apartments, available as late as the 1950s. But Paris was gradually becoming a city of the relatively rich, and in 1970 the figures stood at 2,600,000 and 5,600,000. Cobb refers the reader to Simenon's novel *The Move* for an evocation of the alienation felt by Parisians relocated from the scruffy sociability of working-class Paris to high-rise blocks outside the city.

The Move is one of the best and most harrowing of Simenon's *romans durs*, or serious novels. It was published in 1967, and from today's perspective the move in question seems incom-prehensible. Emile, a clerk in a tourist agency, relocates his family from an apartment in 'old Paris', specifically the rue des Francs Bourgeois in the now trendy and desirable Marais, to a flat in a complex of geometrical new blocks south of the city, near Orly Airport. Emile had disliked the flowered wallpaper he had inherited in his old apartment, as well as its general gloominess and the clutter of the teeming street, and is pleased to be the first occupant of his new block. The one thing the modern reader can identify with is his pleasure at the light-ness of his rooms, which are high in the sky with no nearby obstacles. Also, his new home is on the edge of the countryside and rippling wheat fields, though not for long, because it's soon surrounded by earthmovers 'like monstrous insects lying in wait'. Emile has entered an anonymous world: 'It didn't add up to a village, nor was it a town, and one could hardly speak of a development without losing face.' Sundays are 'without bells'; the TV flickers every time an Orly-bound plane goes past.

Every weekday, Emile drives back into Paris – to the vicinity of his former home, where he still works. Only one Metro station is mentioned: Saint-Paul, on Line 1, which by implication used to be Emile's home station. He parks his car near there. He has no use for the Metro now. In a way, the bleakness of Emile's new situation is more horrific than the violence that takes over at the denouement of the novel.

Richard Cobb describes the destination of these displaced Parisians as *Alphaville*, evoking Jean-Luc Godard's sci-fi film of 1965, a depiction of a dystopian Paris of some vague distant future, although in Godard's noirish vision such Parisian staples as trench coats, beautiful women and incessant smoking are perpetuated.

Cobb always wrote about the Metro with affection, however, even though it too had been created in the name of improved circulation. In his review of Evenson's book, he recalls the year 1935, when he was first in Paris, living on the boulevard Bonne Nouvelle, which runs between the 2nd and 10th Arrondissements, a place of 'lower-echelon' prostitutes, cinemas, flickering neon advertisements and a huge smoking moon face that advertised a patisserie. His flat shook regularly with the rumble of the Metro. Shortly beforehand, as we have seen,

Line 9 had pioneered the Metro extensions of the 1930s, being the first line to cross the city boundary. Perhaps Cobb did not include Metro expansion among the 'follies' of Paris because it tended to *follow* suburban expansion rather than precede and promote it, as the Underground did in London. And when the Metro perpetuated itself, it did so discreetly, usually underground, and always with good taste.

The RER

The continuing expansion of the suburbs prompted a new phase of Metro extension, beginning in 1971 when Line 3 was extended from Gambetta to Gallieni. Congestion on the Metro – especially at Saint-Lazare, where a daily bottleneck occurred as commuters joined the network from suburban lines – prompted the RATP to co-operate with the SNCF to form a regional rail network, the Réseau Express Régional, or RER, which would be separate from the other non-Metro Paris railways. Unlike those other non-Metro lines, the RER would run though the centre of the city, and the RER saved the integrity of the Metro, because without it Metro trains might have had to start skipping stations to reach the suburbs more quickly.

Whereas the Metro lines are designated by numbers, the RER ones have letters, and Lines A and B – forming another *grande croisée*, intersecting at Châtelet-Les Halles – opened in 1977. Today, there are also RER lines C, D and E.

From 2000, the other non-Metro suburban lines were also given letters – HJKLNPUR – and branded as 'Translien', with a pretty leaf motif to emphasise their environmental credentials and counter the supposed stigma of serving the banlieues.

The RER is big. In *The Story of Crossrail*, Christian Wolmar writes that 'the new stations of the RER system were built to a far grander scale than was strictly necessary. This was a cause of some controversy, but was justified by the architectural merit of the stations.' He describes these as 'akin to underground cathedrals, built as single halls housing the two platforms and three times the length of traditional Metro stations. The tunnels, too, were built to larger dimensions than those of the Metro – a prescient course of action, as double-decker trains are now used extensively on the network.' Even so, at peak hours RER trains are packed.

Also in 2000 – and as part of France's national programme of decentralisation – political control of RATP was taken away from the Syndicat des Transports Parisiens (STP), an agent of central government, and transferred to the Syndicat des Transports d'Île de France, or STIF, an unfortunate acronym if you speak English, as indeed is RATP. (Louisa, a formerly English friend of mine who lives in Paris and is proud of having gained French citizenship, tells me that whenever she sees 'RATP' she thinks 'rat trap'.) STIF – which in 2017 began operating as Île de France Mobilités – administers the Parisian transport tax, the Versement Transport, or VT, levied on the salaries of all employees of companies employing more than eleven people. It was introduced in 1973 to fund the RER, and the existence of a hypothecated transport tax in Paris says a lot about the prioritisation of public transport in France.

It is not certain, at the time of writing, that the RATP will operate the Grand Paris Express, even though that is classified as a part of the Metro.

IV

SECOND IMPRESSIONS

Variations on the Vault

In this chapter I want to point out some of the things that the *voyageur*, now schooled in a little Metro history, might notice. It qualifies and develops – but I hope does not undermine – some of my first awestruck impressions. I was particularly impressed by the white station vaults, but not all Metro stations follow the classic template of a wide white vault with two facing platforms and two tracks in between.

Where part of a line had to be constructed close to the surface – to avoid hazards lower down, such as, in sites near the river, the water table – stations might have flat roofs, supported by girders, and these are known as *'tablier métallique'*, or 'metal roof'. These are common on Line 1, including at Gare de Lyon, Champs Élysées-Clemenceau and Palais Royal-Musée du Louvre. The girders run at right angles to the tracks, supporting a series of narrow brick vaults running parallel to the tracks, creating a furrowed effect. These narrow vaults are usually painted white, so in a sense you get more white vaults for your money – albeit small ones – in these stations than in the traditional ones.

The Paris Metro is enthusiastic about its girders. There is no attempt to disguise what they are, and they are spotted with great rivet heads. Admittedly, they are usually painted. At Gare de Lyon, they're yellow; at Champs Élysées-Clemenceau grey; at Palais Royal-Musée du Louvre they are a royal purple. Part of Baker Street Station has a *tablier métallique* similarly arranged, also with purple girders, but it's holding up a roof that's not directly above a platform. As usual, the Parisian version is more dramatic.

The Metro girders are an example of 'public infrastructure expressed', a phrase describing the flamboyance of French engineering I came across in a blog by Simon David called 'La Petite Ceinture and Walks About Paris'. The Petite Ceinture was a railway line built in the 1850s around the course of the Thiers Wall on the edge of Paris, which ploughed its furrow boldly under and over streets, often emerging in open cuttings, at least two of them in public parks. 'The notion of "public infrastructure expressed", particularly with regard to transport, is common throughout Paris,' writes David. Another phrase for the same thing is 'infrastructure porn', which denotes the sometimes bizarre excesses of transport engineering observable in a city (and a country) where *'les ingénieurs'* are given freer rein than in Britain.

There are historical reasons for this. In Britain, an elite education traditionally involved learning the classics; the study of technical subjects was too close to being 'in trade', hence the way British politicians always look embarrassed when donning high-vis vests and hard hats (which they nonetheless do on a regular basis). But in France, home of the École Polytechnique, an elite engineering school, there isn't the same snobbery, and engineers are encouraged to make bolder statements. Simon

David gives the Eiffel Tower and the Pompidou Centre as two examples of this kind of swagger. We will be seeing other instances of it on the Metro, and my own word for it (inspired by 'melodrama') is 'Metro-drama', a flamboyant quality that seems to me to complement, rather than contradict, the essential simplicity of the system.

Most of the *tablier-métallique* stations accommodate the traditional two facing platforms with tracks in between. There are exceptions, and for various reasons: sometimes the Metro narrows down to one track per tunnel, and here there are some single-platform stations. This narrowing might result in the need for offset platforms, as at Liège on Line 12. Where stations are buried very deep, or in poor geology, a central supporting wall might be required between the two tracks, as at Buttes Chaumont on Line 7*bis*. Stations on loops might also have only one platform, and we will be coming to the various types of Metro loop.

All these stations departing from the classic vault are of interest because they're freaks, and we will be visiting some of them. The *voyageur* waiting for a train in these stations is in the position of their counterparts on the London Tube: they are staring at a wall opposite rather than a platform with their fellow humans standing upon it.

Other Station Colours

Anyone curious about the Metro aesthetic I particularly like might care to search online for *Cent Stations du Metro Parisien*, a collection of black and white photographs taken in 1970 by the conceptual artist Daniel Buren.

Buren is a minimalist, interested in repetition (he is known for his paintings of stripes in public places), so it's no surprise he's into the Metro. Each picture is a photograph of a platform taken from the opposite platform; sometimes a train gets in the way, so the opposite platform is compartmentalised in its windows. Where the opposite platform is unobscured, there's always one of the long, rickety wooden benches that used to figure in the stations and that look unnaturally prolonged, like half a dozen park benches bolted together – and like park benches they attracted vagrants who wanted a lie down, hence their eventual removal.

When in Buren's photographs there's only one person sitting on the bench, they look lonely, but the effect is doubly poignant, because they're overwhelmed by the huge poster that often rears up on the station wall immediately behind the bench; and because the pictures were all taken in the same month, the same posters recur: one shows a brand of cheese spread being eaten by a fat boy; another advertises 8 per cent on savings if lodged with BNP. Nobody on the benches looks as if the poster behind was aimed at them. Just one picture is an exception to the prevailing black and white: a photo of Malesherbes station on Line 3, in which it is revealed that the BNP advert is primarily bright yellow, the same colour as the rain mac worn by a woman in the photo, but compared to the others the whole picture looks jarring and wrong, as though hand-coloured, the Metro being such a naturally monochromatic thing. These photographs, by the way, were taken during a period of decline for the Metro, and all the stations seem underlit, the demoralised fluorescent strips illuminating white tiles that look grubby, with the occasional rotting black tooth in among them; but still, there's a melancholic beauty about the scenes.

The pallor of the first Metro stations is expressed in a Metro chase scene in Jean-Pierre Melville's film of 1967, *Le Samouraï*, which is about as close to black-and-white as a colour film can be. Alain Delon is an assassin with a minimalist aesthetic. He inhabits a world largely pale blue and grey. He wears a grey fedora; when looking to steal a car, he contemplates a pale blue Peugeot but settles for a grey Citroen; he lives in a grey flat and smokes Gitanes, whose packets are blue and white, like traditional Metro stations. The chase takes place mainly on Line 11, which had all white stations at the time.

The white vaults were the house style of the Compagnie du Chemin de Fer Metropolitain de Paris, the CMP, which built most of the Metro. The white tiles were possibly copied from the first deep-level, or Tube, line to open in London: the City and South London, which began operations in 1890, and which might have been inspired (if that's the word) to use white tiles by public lavatories. White, anyhow, was intended to alleviate claustrophobia on that very claustrophobic railway, with its narrow tunnel and small, window-less carriages. The CMP style was adopted and refined by the CMP's rival, the Société du Chemin de Fer Électrique Souterrain Nord-Sud de Paris, or Nord-Sud, which built what are today Line 12 and the north part of Line 13.

The Nord-Sud look resembled early CMP style, only more so. White vaults and bevelled tiles formed the basis of it, but the Nord-Sud vaults had straight walls, whereas the CMP stations' walls were curved. Nord-Sud vaults were taller because of the need to accommodate the overhead wires that supplemented the third-rail power supply of the Nord-Sud trains (whereas the CMP ones collected their power entirely from the third rail). The whiteness was offset – and so emphasised – by bands of coloured tiles stretching over the vault, depicting swag patterns on the walls and forming ornate borders for advertising posters. In *U-Bahn, S-Bahn and Tram in Paris*, Christoph Groneck, an author not prone to loose statements, describes Line 12 as 'a gem of transport architecture of the 1910s'. In *Parisians: An Adventure History of Paris*, Graham Robb writes that Nord-Sud was to CMP 'what Maples was to Au Bon Marché or the Ritz to a shelter for homeless'.

A detailed discussion of the Nord-Sud style would become an account of Lines 12 and 13, so I will defer that until we come to the chapter on the individual lines. Let's say for now that original Nord-Sud tiling survives at Pasteur, Solférino and Porte de La Chapelle on Line 12; at Liège and La Fourche on Line 13. Several stations on 12 and 13 have reproduction Nord-Sud. On many ex-Nord-Sud stations, and a few of those of the CMP, white tiles were covered over by the first major departure from white-vault purity, a style called *carrossage*.

*

Carrossage means 'covering'. The casual traveller will notice that at some stations the walls of the vault have been covered by metallic panelling. There are so few of these today that they are a pleasant novelty when spotted, but *carrossage* of various colours – though mainly yellow – was applied at about eighty stations between 1965 and 1974; it once challenged the white-vault regime, and if it had succeeded, I would not be writing this book.

In the typical *carrossage* style, station names were written on a brown background in a gloomy parchment yellow, as though anticipating the nicotine-staining likely to occur in those days when you could smoke on Metro platforms. One motivation was to cover up rotting white tiles, so there's something unwholesome about *carrossage*, like a person wearing too much make-up. Another was to create, at those beautiful ex-Nord-Sud stations, advertising panels of a smaller size, equivalent to those on the CMP stations, which had become standard. (The small Nord-Sud panels were not being used, so that the stations resembled art galleries where a heist had occurred, and the Metro needed to boost advertising revenue, to help fund its suburban extensions.) Most stations on today's Lines 12 and the north part of 13 received *carrossage*. The last time I was at Marx Dormoy station on Line 12, the red *carrossage* was being removed and the white tiles beneath were revealed, looking in perfectly good condition. I could imagine the workmen ripping away the *carrossage* in anger, indignant at what it had been concealing these past fifty years. On the other hand, maybe we have to thank *carrossage* for protecting the tiles. Classic, intact carrossage in all its jaundiced glory survives at Falguière on Line 12.

There is a modern, stylised version of *carrossage* on the Line 11 platforms at Arts et Métiers. The covering is suggestive of burnished, riveted copper, with portholes in which things like globes, compasses and other tokens of nineteenth-century intellectualism seem to be spookily floating. Clearly, you are in Captain Nemo's submarine, which has dived deep, if the dim lighting is anything to go by. The effect – designed to promote the museum of engineering above the station – is beautifully created, and what makes it more admirable is its sheer whimsicality, in that the typical tourist passing through is likely to experience this station as some inexplicable mirage.

At Parmentier on Line 3, there is another stylised version of *carrossage* with the covering resembling a garden trellis, appropriate for this agriculturally themed station, which celebrates – try not to get too excited – the potato, as promoted by that vegetable's number one champion, Antoine-Augustin Parmentier.

There are twenty or so special, themed stations on the Metro, and if Arts et Métiers is the biggest production number, Parmentier is at the other end of the scale, being more like a school assembly presentation. When I first read its illustrated panels, the primary one heralding '*La fabuleuse aventure de la pomme de terre*', I wondered whether this was a joke. The seats at the station, which are shaped like tractor seats, reinforce the notion. There does seem to be a Department of Humour, or similar, lurking in the Maison de la RATP. It goes in for

April Fool jokes employing wordplay that I, with my appalling French, would never spontaneously appreciate if just passing through, and the charm of which, I fear, is about to be lost in translation, but here goes. On April Fool's Day 2016, RATP changed the name of Télégraphe station on Line 11 to '#TWEET'. Readers might detect the adjacency of terminology here, but perhaps the gag needs more explanation. It will be discussed further – and drained of any possible remaining ribaldry – when we come to discuss Line 11. Here's another, easier to grasp: at the time of the 2022 World Cup, Argentine Station on Line 1, so named in honour of a visit to Paris by Eva Perón in 1948, was temporarily re-named after Argentina's opponents in the final: France; and it must have been painful to restore the earlier name, France having lost on penalties.

The next aesthetic innovation was called Mouton-Duvernet, after the Line 4 station to which it was first applied in 1968. Basically, Mouton-Duvernet was the application of flat tiles of various shapes, and – to paraphrase Henry Ford – you could have them in any colour you liked as long as it was orange. Orange was a very Sixties colour in that it did not often occur in nature. It was psychedelic, and clearly RATP thought this would make its stations groovy. Every so often, the traveller will see an orange wall on the Metro – usually just a quick flash in a corridor – and, if they are old enough, they will be transported back to their bell-bottomed youth.

The style, applied to about twenty stations between 1968

and 1973, has been almost entirely banished from the Metro platforms, but it survives at Montparnasse on Line 6, at Charles de Gaulle Étoile on the same line, and at Havre-Caumartin on Line 9, where the seats are also orange, and I really do feel I've been 'Tangoed'. What's touching about this station is that the tiles come in various shades of orange, as if the designers kept re-committing to the colour, quite unable to think of a better one. There are also orange tiles – small ones, about the dimensions of upright playing cards – at the Line 2 platforms at Nation.

There are, incidentally, some walls of orange tiles off the Piccadilly Line platforms at South Kensington Station in London – fitting, perhaps, given that there's a kind of French colony around there. I asked a man working at the barrier in South Ken when these tiles had been put in. 'Must have been the Sixties,' he said. 'I was a boy then, and my bedroom was the same colour.' I know a late middle-aged couple who live near Oberkampf Metro station, and I asked them if it was true that the Line 5 platforms there had once been orange. They looked at each other, frowning, trying to recollect, and then they both laughed and said yes.

The style that followed Mouton-Duvernet is evinced in about a hundred stations. It was applied between 1974 and 1986, and it's called Andreu-Motte, after the design team of Joseph-André Motte and Paul Andreu. It represents a partial coming to terms with the original whiteness of stations, but it evinced a continuing feeling that they were too pallid. White was allowed to remain the main colour, but the bevelled tiles were often replaced with flat ones, and colour was introduced in the form, first, of a light fitting suspended above the full length of the platform, like a series of window boxes containing fluorescent tubes. The colour of this fitting matched the colour of a tiled ledge on the platform, on which were fixed brightly coloured moulded enamel seats of the types that might have been called 'Space Age' in the 1960s and Seventies. These replaced the rickety, long wooden benches, and Joseph-André Motte, being a Frenchman, described the change in philosophical (and somewhat sexist) terms. A man, he stated, 'has his wealth: he needs a seat of his own. Whether this individual is cultured or whether he can neither read nor write, he is a character. Christians will say that it is the child of God. Others will say it is an original spirit, it is unique. Two men are not alike. So the single seat.' The quotation is from a book called *Questions(s) design* (and I have transcribed the title correctly) by Christine Colin.

There are a handful of wooden benches of the traditional, rudimentary park-bench type left on the Metro – not as long as the originals, but still capable of supporting a sleeping homeless person. See for, example, those at Solférino or at Chemin Vert on Line 8, where (in a clash with the station name) they are purple. There are several black and white photographs of the old benches that the Andreu-Motte style displaced in a book I own called *Metro de Paris*, published in 1969, and so minimal that no author or editor's name is given. The *voyageurs* on the benches exhibit the wide range of clothing that characterised the 1960s. Everyone looks either modern or old-fashioned: a man in a bow tie, for example, sits next to a woman in a miniskirt.

I recommend this book, which also has shots of train interiors: lonely-looking people – even though they are often beautiful women – sitting on the wooden seats of the Sprague stock. The photographer takes care to include the various warning signs displayed in the carriages, which to my eyes look more formal than probably intended. One warns 'LES AUTEURS DE GRAFFITI' of fines; another counsels that it is an offence to press the emergency alarm button 'SANS MOTIF PLAUSIBLE'. The most famous, or infamous (if you were a smoker) sign was 'DÉFENSE DE FUMER ET DE CRACHER': no smoking or spitting, the latter injunction an attempt to stop the spread of tuberculosis.

There are so many stations in the Andreu-Motte style (at one point about a third of the network) that any tourist might take it to be the typical Metro look. I tend to like or dislike it according to the colour chosen. I like the blue at Ledru Rollin on Line 8 – only, perhaps, because the blue complements the white in the same way as on the original Metro stations.

Andreu-Motte was succeeded by the Ouï-Dire style, implemented at about thirty stations in the mid-1980s, and usually still extant. It involves a new light housing, retained by supports resembling scythes. From these, lights are projected through coloured filters onto the white vault roofs, giving a subtle Northern Lights effect. The colour of what I would like to call the 'lampshades', but which are usually referred to by the workaday term 'light housings', varies between stations, but always matches the poster frames and seats (no longer placed on ledges, since these had been used as beds by the tramps displaced from the old benches).

You can see Ouï-Dire at Odéon on Line 10, where the purples, greens and golds on the roof are pleasantly Christmassy. The light fixture, poster frames and seats here are yellow. At Château Landon on Line 7, the light fitting, seats and poster frames are red. The coloured lights on the roof are similar to, but not the same as, those at Odéon. No two Ouï-Dire displays are the same, and this is the style's appeal: the mystery. Ouï-Dire, by the way, means 'hearsay', implying something apprehended indirectly and subjectively. It's a station design that invites you to use your imagination, but then again so did the purely white stations of 1900, because any sort of electric light applied to the white bevelled tiles created a mesmerising, pearlescent shimmer that early *voyageurs* would have interpreted, according to their mood, as uplifting or melancholic.

After decades of experimentation, the Metro seems to have come round to this way of thinking, because since 1999 the Renouveau du Metro programme has been restoring white bevelled tiles to the many stations where they were lost entirely or decaying in situ. Andreu-Motte and Ouï-Dire stations in good condition will be spared; *carrossage* and Mouton-Duvernet ones are doomed.

The restored whiteness has been rolled out in conjunction with a new light fitting, designed by Bruno Gaudin. It is attached directly to the start of the curvature of the vault, rather than being pendant from it, so it emphasises that curvature. White with greyish supports, like chicken meat against chicken bones, the Bruno Gaudin light is self-effacing; it doesn't introduce another colour. On the ex-Nord-Sud stations, the standard fixture might block out decorative detailing on the vault roof, so a narrower, more tubular version was developed. At the time of writing the implementation of Renouveau du Metro is particularly evident along Line 4. Here and elsewhere it is being applied in conjunction with a new type of plastic seat: the *coque* or shell seats, shaped like half-cockleshells. These do introduce new colours to the entire system, and very wittily. My wife, a more visual person than me, was stopped in her tracks by some shell seats at Marcadet Poissoniers on Line 12. 'Mint!' she exclaimed.

Guimard in Context

In a letter of 1886 to the Ministry of Public Works, Charles Garnier, architect of the neo-Baroque Paris Opéra, wrote, 'The Metropolitan Railroad, in the eyes of most Parisians, will only be excused if it rejects absolutely all industrial character so as to be completely a work of art. Paris must not be made into a factory, it must stay a museum.'

Garnier had been one of the 'Committee of 300' who'd opposed the 'useless and monstrous' Eiffel Tower – one objector for each metre of the proposed structure. Alexandre Dumas was another. Responding in *Le Temps* on 14 February 1887, Gustave Eiffel himself suggested that 'the essential lines of a monument are determined by its perfect accord with its purpose,' a good definition of 'infrastructure expressed'.

The stakes were high when, in 1900, the CMP organised a competition to find a design for the Metro entrances. It is said that the competition was won by a man who hadn't entered it: Hector Guimard, who had become famous as the architect of an Art Nouveau fantasia, Castel Béranger, an apartment block at 14 rue Lafontaine in the up-and-coming 16th Arrondissement (we will be visiting Castel Béranger when we come to the Metro line that serves it). Adrien Bénard, president of the CMP, admired the building, which had been completed in 1898, and he commissioned Guimard for the Metro.

Guimard, a considerable self-publicist, was riding a big wave. Art Nouveau had been a dominant theme at the Paris Exposition of 1900. Romanticism and modernity went hand in hand on the Metro, and Art Nouveau itself was seemingly timeless: looking back towards natural forms in reaction against Beaux Arts monumentalism, and forward in its willingness to use modern building materials like iron, glass, ceramics and concrete. Perhaps it seemed to Bénard that Art Nouveau would meet Garnier's criterion of being 'anti-industrial', but Guimard's work would provoke the architectural grandees of the Second Empire.

Even today, his *entourages* (station entrances), surmounted by those great iron flowers, look extreme, and where they survive, they have been modified only in one small way. Today, Guimard *entourages* have a placard below the lamps featuring a map of the Metro on one side and an advert on the other. Fixed to the top of the map is the station name, all done in a commensurate style; but when the Guimards first appeared there was only the word 'Metropolitain' on a board suspended between the two lamp-flowers, the typeface having been created by Guimard, with the two Ts and the P taller than the other letters, as though shading them like trees in a forest. When I asked Julian Pepinster why the name of the station was not originally displayed, he shrugged and said: 'You were Parisian; you *knew* where you were.'

What would the first Metro users have expected to find below these entrances? Surely something cosily reminiscent of a rabbit warren, rather than the glacial whiteness that actually awaited? It's hard to know which would be the stranger, and that there is somehow harmony between them must be something to do with what Lawrence Osborne, in his *Paris Dreambook*, called the Metro's 'innate tendency towards dream'.

The second most common type of Guimard entrance after the flowers resembled a beautiful bus shelter, with a fanned-out frosted glass roof veined with iron supports and (sometimes) walls of frosted glass and orange iron panels. There were seven of these, and they were known as *édicules* or kiosks (the exoticism of that word being very seductive to fin-de-siècle Europeans). They were also referred to as '*libellules*', the French word for dragonflies, because their roofs resemble dragonfly wings. Only two survive. One is at Porte Dauphine at the western, or posher, end of Line 2. It stands in a small park (a sort of little annex to the Bois de Boulogne) next to a busy road, as if it really were an organic phenomenon. Anyone loitering here for ten minutes is practically guaranteed to see someone turning up to photograph the kiosk. The other survivor is on Line 12 at Abbesses, where it was moved from Hôtel de Ville station in 1974. (You can see it on the cover of this book.) Abbesses is a Nord-Sud station, and Guimard worked for the CMP, so Abbesses would never have had a kiosk originally. The Nord-Sud entrances were dignified but unspectacular: green railings rising from light brown terracotta staircase walls, with the word 'Metropolitain' in white on a red background, the letters having a self-deprecatory stencilled effect.

The Hôtel de Ville kiosk was moved to Abbesses to make way for an underground car park. It's appreciated there, Abbesses being in picturesque Montmartre, popular with tourists. A third kiosk of the Guimard type forms one of the many entrances to Châtelet station (the one in Place Sainte-Opportune), but this is a fake, or to be more polite a replica, created in 2000 to celebrate the Metro centenary.

Lastly, there were Guimard's three pagodas or pavilions – street-level buildings involving a lot of glass, so they resembled winter gardens. They had waiting rooms and were in effect stations. One was at Bastille, and two were at Étoile – both on Line 1. Photographs survive of the one at Bastille, considered Guimard's most flamboyant work, and his masterpiece: it looked extremely Japanese, except for the curvature of the canopy over the entrance (whose double doors were accommodated within a large 'M' motif). This disproportionately large canopy reminds me of the peak of a baseball cap, but I can't

believe it reminded the *voyageurs* of anything at all. In the photographs, the top-hatted and long-skirted individuals coming
and going from it seem preposterously stolid and conventional
in comparison with the building.

Guimard planted his exotic seeds across Paris between 1900
and 1912, and they divided opinion. *Le Temps* criticised the
'disorderly hieroglyphics' of Guimard's lettering. *Le Figaro*
spoke of 'contorted ramps and hunchbacked lamp posts', but
Art Nouveau in France began to be spoken of in relaxed terms
as 'Le style Metro', and it remained fashionable for the next
twenty years or so.

Other Entrances

Guimard began his long slide out of favour in 1904, when his
design for an entrance to Opéra station, which opened that year
on Line 3, was rejected, on the grounds it would not 'harmonise' with Charles Garnier's Opera House. 'Will we henceforth
have to harmonise the station at Père Lachaise with the cemetery and construct it in the form of a tomb?' he demanded in
La Presse. 'Will we harmonise that of the Place Mazas with the
Morgue?' (His iron flowers at Père Lachaise definitely do not
harmonise with the graveyard.)

Garnier was dead by now, but the defenders of his opera house
believed its dignity would be affronted by one of Guimard's
outbreaks of jungly ironwork, and no doubt these academicians
would have been appalled by the famous photograph of the

excavation in Place de l'Opéra, showing the arch of the Line 3 tunnel like a bone exposed during surgery. They must have wished the golden winged figures on the roof of the Opéra could have flown it away to some safer location.

The job of designing a Metro entrance for Opéra – and other places too dignified for Guimards – was given to Joseph Cassien-Bernard, who created a sober, neo-classical entrance composed of little more than a low stone balustrade. There's one at Place de la Concorde, immediately outside the €1,500-a-night Crillon Hotel. It leads to Concorde station, but you wouldn't know it until you'd descended the steps and walked along the corridor to the ticket hall. The only indication that this *entourage* serves public transport is the word 'Metropolitain' regretfully carved in small letters on the balustrade, and with an angularity that refutes Guimard's typeface. The entrance is beautiful in its way, with two lanterns glowing goldenly, but I wonder how many guests at the Crillon have deigned to walk down those steps. (This, I think, is the entrance by which the character Jules descends into the Metro on his moped while being pursued by the police in Jean-Jacques Beineix's 1981 film *Diva*. He then rides the bike down more stairs than are at Concorde, so this bit must have been filmed at one of the deeper stations. Next thing you know, he's at Opéra station, then riding along one of the moving walkways at Châtelet. I suspect that walkway was chosen for its red tiles. It's interesting that *Diva*, like *Subway*, which was made four years later, favours the colourised Metro. Both films were in the visually striking, almost cartoonish, style of the Cinema du Look movement, and I suppose workaday white Metro tunnels represented the social realism on which Cinema du Look had turned its back.)

Post-Guimard, Metro entrances generally became more sensible: a matter of straight, green iron railings, topped by a signpost or *candélabre*. The original versions of these are said to be in the Val d'Osne style, after the iron foundry where they were manufactured, and they look much more old-fashioned than the Guimards they replaced. They consisted of a backlit sign reading 'Metro' (note abbreviation), the letters white on red, with the same stencilled effect that the Nord-Sud was using, as if the letters had been cut by a train running over them. The sign was mounted in an ornately embellished cast-iron frieze with a luminous, milky white globe above.

From 1924, the Val d'Osne signposts gave way to the plainer 'Dervaux' style of the 1930s, named after their designer, Adolphe Dervaux. Many Dervaux signposts remain; the Val d'Osne ones are rarer. There's one outside St Paul station on Line 1; another stands at one of the entrances to St Michel station in Place St André des Arts. This little square (a haven away from all the confusion of St Michel's bloated neighbour, St Michel-Notre Dame, which serves the RER) could hardly be more Parisian. The station entrance offsets its Val d'Osne lamp with a Guimard railing sans flowers. Another antique street lamp is thrown in nearby for good measure. There's also a café with terrace, a Morris column, a *tabac* and a *bureau de change*, where I used to stock up on francs before burrowing deeper into the bars of the Sixth.

In the 1950s, the lamps gave way to what were essentially totems or logos rather than lamps, although they were still lit up at nights. In the late 1930s a large, red letter 'M' inside a blue circle appeared outside Sentier and Denfert-Rochereau stations. Running horizontally through the 'M' was the word 'METRO' written on a blue bar. (And there was no acute accent over the 'E', by the way. The acute accent never has appeared on Metro signposts or logos; nor did it appear when, on the earlier signs, 'Metropolitain' was written in full.) The combination of circle and crossbar looked very like the London roundel, and 'this similarity was probably the downfall of the crossbar,' suggests Mark Ovenden in *Paris Metro Style*. The Metro totems and logos evolved through various forms and colours of Ms in circles. By the 1970s, the standard totem was a luminous yellow M bounded by two steel rings. This looks, apparently deliberately, like a radio or TV aerial. Lately, a blue M inside what looks like a white-infilled squash racquet has begun to appear.

Guimard's pavilion at Bastille was demolished in 1962. Many of his *entourages* had gone by then, and his pagoda at Étoile had been knocked down as early as 1926. Art Nouveau had over-stayed its welcome, and Paris was tired of it. The figure usually given is that of 141 entrances designed by Guimard, eighty-six survive. A British antique-dealer friend of mine who's in his seventies recalls that, in the mid-1960s, 'There was a salvage place in Paris where you could buy Guimard entrances – the railings, the two lamps and nameplate. They weren't exactly cheap, because Guimard was very important, even if out of fashion. You'd probably have to pay about six thousand pounds, or sixty thousand francs, for one. But then you could sell it for a lot more to an American Art Nouveau collector . . . or you could put it up in your garden.'

Art Nouveau, incidentally, was not only 'Le Style Metro', it was also, to a lesser extent, the style of the London Underground. The architect of the tubes built by the American mogul Charles Tyson Yerkes was a mysterious young man called Leslie Green, who had lived in Paris in the 1890s. He designed the oxblood-tiled surface buildings mentioned above, and his work can be seen in the interiors of the stations that today form the central parts of the Northern Line (West End branch), the Piccadilly and the Bakerloo. The Art Nouveau touches are in the bottle-green tiling and dado rails decorated with acanthus or pomegranate leaves – see Regent's Park, for instance – and the ticket window surrounds at, say, Hampstead, or in the *depictions* of ticket windows in tiles used to frame messages like 'No Exit' or 'Way Out' at various Yerkes stations. Leslie Green – who looked like a Frenchman, with his haughty face and carefully combed moustache – died aged thirty-three in 1908, possibly from over overwork.

Hector Guimard died in New York, in relative obscurity, in 1942. He and his wife, being Jewish, had left Paris on the eve of the war, and it was in New York that his artistic rehabilitation began, in 1970, when the Museum of Modern Art staged an exhibition of his work, and there is to this day a Guimard *entourage* there.

*

Some Metro stations do have surface buildings. For example, the entrance to St Jacques station on Line 6 is an attractive brick kiosk dating from 1906 with Guimard lettering above the endearingly narrow domestic-scale doors (two Sortie, one Entrée). The idea, perhaps, was to provide customers with momentary shelter from rain and cold on their way to the trains, the station being in an open cutting below. The entrance to Palais Royal-Musée du Louvre station at Place Colette resembles either a tangle of bead necklaces, a crown or an ornate bird cage. (It would make a large bird cage, but it's small for a station entrance.) It's called Kiosque (that word again) des Noctambules, and it was designed by Jean-Michel Othoniel in 2000 for the Metro centenary. The last time, I looked, some hooligan had jammed a shopping trolley in between the kiosk and the lacy, silvery bench seat that goes with it. '*Noctambules*', by the way, means 'sleepwalkers'.

I once exited Riquet station on Line 7 to find myself emerging from what was in effect the ground floor of an apartment block, and moreover an estate agent's sign announced that the flat directly above the exit was available to rent. If the agents were not advertising the apartment as 'convenient for the Metro' they were missing a trick.

The Evolution of the Trains

When I spoke of the greenness of the early trains – the Spragues – I was slightly over-simplifying, because one of the

carriages was always red: the first-class one. Whether this
fascinated me back in the early Seventies I can't recall, but
it does now. In a post of 4 December 2014, a travel website
called Messy Nessy ('Don't be a tourist') suggested that the
class system on the Metro, abolished under Socialist President
Mitterrand as late as 1991, was 'what most distinguished it
from all other subways of the world'. I don't think that's true;
what most distinguishes the Metro is its beauty. But first class
certainly is rare on modern metros.

A class system did flicker on the London Underground,
primarily on the Metropolitan Railway, the Paris Metro's
etymological forebear. Its platforms had overhanging signs
indicating where the first-class carriages would stop, just as
the Metro once did. The short-lived Great Northern & City
Railway (aka 'the Big Tube') also had classes – but classes had
disappeared from the Underground and all other trains operating solely within central London by 1941. The war was on,
and Londoners were supposedly 'all in it together', a claim that
could not be made in wartime France – and in occupied Paris,
German soldiers used first class without paying. For paying
customers, first class has generally cost 80 per cent as much
again as second, which was still not very much, the Metro
having always been cheap. On the Sprague trains, first class had
seats upholstered quite minimally in leather, whereas second-
class seats were wooden, albeit attractively so, with dark and
light slats alternating.

When the Spragues began to be replaced by trains
that were not green, but mainly blue, first-class cars were

cream-coloured. Later, first class was denoted by a yellow strip on the carriage exterior. From 1982, the first-class carriage was open to anyone before 9 a.m. and after 5 p.m., to mitigate rush-hour overcrowding, so it was fading by then, and the apparent clash with '*liberté, égalité, fraternité*' was perhaps always illusory. First class wasn't necessarily used by the rich; it also catered to people who wanted, or needed, to be sure of a seat. It was like the Parisian choice between drinking while standing at the bar (*au comptoir*) and sitting at a table (*en salle*). Did we Martins sit in first back in the 1970s? I don't think so; I seem to remember a hot, wooden environment. My sister also thinks we sat on wooden seats, because she recalls a contrast between the old-fashionedness of the train and the Seventies chic of a woman passenger who wore jeans and ankle-length suede boots. The other day, I found a Metro ticket in an old wallet of mine. It dated from the early 1980s, when Metro tickets were yellow. It's crudely stamped with a big '2'.

Rail enthusiasts, by the way, would avoid first because it was in the middle of the train: the second of four or the third of five carriages. They preferred to travel in the front carriage so they could watch the driver and the oncoming track through the glass bulkhead (the window between the carriage and the driver's cab). There was no 'dead man's handle' on the Spragues, by which the train would be stopped if the driver collapsed, so he had to be visible to the guard, who also travelled in the front car.

There is still a glass window between the passengers and the driver on most Metro trains, but the glass is smoked. This is because the tunnel is dimly lit, and the driver's view of its important signal lights and other potential hazards would be impeded if he were flooded with light from behind – a consideration that for some reason did not apply in the Sprague days. On a modern Metro train, if you stand close to the smoked glass and squint, you can see the driver as a ghostly dark outline and the hypnotically recurring lights of the tunnel beyond. I have never heard a satisfactory explanation of why there is any window at all these days, given that there are no guards on the trains, but perhaps the glass is there so that *passengers* can verify that the driver is alive and well. On Lines 1, 4 and 14, however, we are back to square one: passengers can have a driver's-eye view because there *are* no drivers.

Metro trains were electric from the start – that is, from 1900 when anyone wanting to use electricity on a large scale had to build their own power station. The Metro's was on the Quai de la Rapée, on the North Bank of the river in east Paris. It was adjacent to the headquarters of CMP, which was a Gothic chateau-like building, demolished in 1995 to make way for Maison de la RATP, HQ of the current operator. The power station was decommissioned in 1927, when the electrical requirements of the Metro evolved in some way beyond my comprehension. You can see its chimneys in the background of a couple of shots in the above-mentioned crime film, *Rififi*; they are not smoking, because the power station was about to be demolished. Today, electricity from various sources (including abroad) is delivered to seven RATP power stations across Paris, from where it's distributed to about 200 substations. Some historic ones remain in service, and of course they're beautiful. If you go to Bastille station and exit at boulevard Henri IV, you will see one of them on boulevard Bourdon. It looks like a sort of Spanish castle, with the enormous metal-framed semi-circular window standing in for a raised drawbridge. A commemorative plaque announces it as 'Sous Station Électrique Bastille 1900'.

The Metro uses third-rail electrification. That is, the trains collect their power from a third rail alongside the running rails, which is the standard method of operating electric railways. The London Underground uses third and fourth rail. I asked an engineer who has worked as a consultant to the London Underground and other world metros to explain the historical origins of London's fourth-rail system; his answer reinforced the idea that British railway building was not quite the undirected free-for-all of caricature.

'It was originally adopted for the District Railway, since it was considered likely the Board of Trade would prevent widespread use of a three-rail system so close to the surface in central London, because of the risk of interference with sensitive government telephonic equipment. An added advantage of the system was that it would keep voltage losses to a minimum and allow wider spacing of substations.'

The Nord-Sud company used third rail in combination with overhead wire, to allow wider spacing of substations. The Nord-Sud also had its own version of the Spragues, and its trains, like its stations, were prettier than those of the CMP. They looked old-fashioned even when first unveiled. Carriages were light yellow and red for first class, duck-egg blue and grey for second, with classical border designs, and the classes indicated by Roman numerals. In the carriage interiors, filigree effects were cut into the metal above the windows, and the brass luggage racks were ornate. The *strapontins*, or folding seats, near the doors were as minimally elegant as shooting sticks. The Nord-Sud company didn't persist long enough to witness the era of the Metro trains with tyres, the *matériel pneu* (MP) as opposed to *matériel fer* (MF): the two types are known by those initials followed by two digits denoting the year of design. The oldest trains currently operating, for example, are the MP59s on Line 11, and they are not long for this world.

Trains with tyres are on Lines 1, 4, 6 and 14. I have already mentioned the reasons for their introduction: faster acceleration and braking, reduced noise. In his *Paris Metro Handbook*, Brian Hardy calls the tyred trains 'an unqualified success', and Hardy knows his stuff, having worked for London Underground for many years. But the consultant engineer I quoted above is bemused by the *matériel pneu*: 'They're an answer looking for a question,' he told me, by which he meant, first, that they do not justify their expense. After all, the technology is complex and involved: the tyred wheels, which run on reinforced concrete strips alongside the steel running rails, need lateral steel guide wheels to keep them in alignment; the trains are also fitted with conventional steel wheels, normally kept raised above the running rails, but which descend onto them should a puncture occur. His second implication was that French railway engineers like novelty for its own sake; that they tend to show off, to be 'flashy', a notion that chimes in with 'infrastructure expressed'.

The RATP sold rubber-tyred trains to Montreal, Mexico City and Santiago, so they can't be *that* weird, and they ran in operational service in Britain during the 1930s. In 1932 Michelin sent a tyre-shod railcar with a Renault engine over from France on the Night Ferry (the cross-Channel train ferry) as part of a UK promotion. The car was put into service on the Southern Railway, running between Ascot, Aldershot and Alton. Others followed elsewhere, and they were popular with passengers for the smoothness of the ride, but they were too far off the mainstream to be widely adopted.

In Paris, it was thought the tyred trains had had their day after the third generation of them, the MP73s, were introduced for Line 6, where they can still be seen, treading softly on the many viaducts of that line. But tyres made a comeback when MP89 became the rolling stock of the Metro's futuristic showpiece, Line 14, when it opened in 1998. Some railway traditionalists object to the tyres – not only for making the trains too car-like, but also for making the wrong sound. Trains ought to be clangourous, not muffled. And can rubber-shod trains be called part of *chemin de fer*? Tyres do give trains a certain buoyancy, justifying the Metro's habit of referring dreamily to passengers as *'voyageurs'* in its public address announcements.

✳

I feel more like an abstracted *voyageur* late at night on a quiet backwater line like *3bis* than I do in rush hour on Line 1, whose automatic trains arrive at the stations every 85 seconds.

I generally do prefer the older Metro trains, like the MP59s of Line 11 or the MF67s on Lines 3, *3bis*, 10 and 12. They are – viewed from inside – simple, cream-coloured steel boxes, amusingly reminiscent of garden outhouses, because they have ladders propped up at the carriage ends. Since the Metro is an underground phenomenon, you'd think these ladders were for climbing up; in fact, they're for climbing down. They have hooks at the top corresponding to holes beneath the doors of the carriages. If the carriage needs to be evacuated, *voyageurs* can descend to the side of the tracks using them. All the Metro trains have ladders, but they're not visible on the later stocks, perhaps being secreted under seats. The staff know where they are, of course. The tunnels being vaults and not tubes, there is room to evacuate the carriages in this manner. One of the reasons the Metro has fully automatic driverless trains on three lines and the London Underground doesn't have any is this ability to remove passengers from a stricken automatic train.

At the time of writing, the driverless trains are on lines 1, 4 and 14, and small children are drawn to the front of these like filings to the end of a magnet. (The same phenomenon occurs on the automated Docklands Light Railway in London, whose tall, thin trains are reminiscent of Metro trains.) They like to sit at the windscreen and pretend to be driving, in which they are indulged by RATP, which provides mock control boards labelled *'Conduite reservée aux enfants'* or similar. Nonetheless,

I have elbowed children out of the way in order to gain a front seat.

By the way, a Francophobe friend of mine once chuntered: 'French unions are so militant they erect barricades of burning tyres in the streets. How come they agreed to having driverless trains?' It's true that French trains of all types are strike-prone, which is why I recommend not buying tickets online, because it's hard to get a refund. I once had to spend a night on a sleeper train parked at Gare d'Austerlitz that was supposed to be travelling to the French Riviera. I was provided with a sort of Red Cross parcel of emergency supplies kept on hand for just such regular events, and whereas I've hardly ever been inconvenienced by a signalling problem on the Metro, I've been incommoded by a strike many times. It's a strike, of course, that keeps young Zazie from being 'Dans Le Metro' in Raymond Queneau's novel. It is explained to her that the Metro 'has fallen asleep under the ground, for the employees with their perforating punches have ceased to work'. But Metro strikes are about money, not redundancies. A job on the Metro is highly secure, and any driver displaced by driverless technology has been redeployed elsewhere.

Most of the Metro lines that *apparently* have drivers are not really being driven by a human at all, because ATO, or Automatic Train Operation, applies. By ATO (which is not the same as full automation), the driver merely starts the train after a station stop, ensuring that all passengers are safely aboard. ATO is more widespread on the Metro than on the London Underground, and the Metro is hurtling towards full automation. Over the next half-dozen years, it will displace many of the older trains described here.

A Note on Tickets

When I began writing this book, I fantasised that some fortuitous bang on the head, or a session of hypnosis, might bring that Seventies Metro ride back to me. Were our tickets punched by a *poinçonneur* or *poinçonneuse* – a man or woman sitting at the entrance to the platform, either in a little booth or on a spartan wooden chair?

Serge Gainsbourg had his first hit, in 1958, with a song called *'Le Poinçonneur des Lilas'*, whose bustling chorus – suggestive of a fast Metro train – repeatedly mentions the word *trou*, meaning a hole. A Scopitone film was made of Gainsbourg performing it – that is, a film that could be played on a special sort of jukebox – which can now be seen on YouTube. Gainsbourg sits in his booth, amid darkly glittering Metro scenes; illuminated signs, seen approaching and receding as from a train, have a lunar glow. The images suggest night, but that might not be the case, and the song's theme is the unnaturalness of this subterranean world. Gainsbourg looks profoundly sad as he punches tickets passed to him by people whose faces we never see. Like a puppy, he doesn't seem to have grown into his large features, although perhaps this is the effect of his crew cut of the time. The punched-out bits of card (the opposite of holes) accumulate on his winkle-picker shoes; sometimes, apparently, they would be caught up in the breeze made by a departing train, like confetti thrown at nobody in particular.

Among the montage of illuminated signs is one reading 'Porte des Lilas', and it's possible that the ticket-punching scenes were filmed there. We are going to be visiting that interesting station, which for a few years was the terminus of Line 11 and still is the terminus of that anomalous runt, line 3*bis*.

In *Footprints in Paris*, Gillian Tindall writes that 'the *poinçonneuses* were proverbially ill-tempered. They knitted, to pass the otherwise dreary, draughty hours, and occasionally two on opposite platforms would hold loud, complaining conversations across the rails.' They controlled a gate – a *'portillon'* – through which they could work off some of their aggression in the name of controlling passenger flow. During rush hour, they would drag the gate across the platform entrances as the train came into the platform. 'You had to get to the platform before it [the train] was actually in,' writes Tindall. 'The Metro authority seemed to have a fixed fear – eventually abandoned – of people trying to jump into the train at the last moment.' A *poinçonneur* (that is, a male ticket checker) adds to the tension in the final chase scene of the film *Charade*, by demanding to see the ticket of Cary Grant (who hasn't got one) as he pursues Audrey Hepburn (who has). The pair, by the way, enter the Metro at St Jacques station on Line 6, but then they are immediately on Line 1, and they exit the Metro at Palais Royal on that line.

The last *poinçonneurs* disappeared in 1974, replaced by the automatic ticket barriers you often see people leaping over, or going through two at a time in a co-ordinated shuffle.

Sometimes they shuffle through immediately behind me, and I feel like a tourist-mug. At Gare du Nord, I once saw a window cleaner leap the barrier while carrying his ladder and bucket. The assumption seems to be that the Metro is so cheap, it might as well be free. But the paradox is that if you are caught on the system without a ticket, you are dealt with severely: an on-the-spot fine of 40 euros. This is why all *voyageurs* should retain their tickets throughout the journey.

Card tickets are due to be phased out in 2025. Every year, 550 million are bought, which represents 50 million tons of paper, most of which is presumably not recycled, because (except for a few cases where the Metro shares a station with the RER) you don't have to put the tickets into a barrier at the end of your journey – a function of the flat fare, which is a component of the system's elegance. Instead, you just batter your way through a sturdy glass door and skip up a few steps into another beautiful street.

When smoking was legal in French bars, you would see Metro tickets stubbed out, as it were, alongside the fag butts in ash trays. Some tickets do seem to want to gravitate back to the place of their origin, because you see them lying on the ledges or baffle plates immediately beneath the Metro ventilation grilles that are all over central Paris. There's a large one at Place d'Acadie just off boulevard St Germain. At these sites the Metro, only a few feet below, exhales warm air, which is why homeless people pitch their tents on the grilles. In rue de l'Ancienne Comédie in the 6th Arrondissement there are a succession of small grilles, atop Line 10, each about 4 feet by

4, and one cold evening when I was passing, all were occupied by sitters clutching bottles of booze, riding their own personal magic carpets (and there was nothing comedic about the sight, of course, in spite of the street's name).

The original CMP tickets were pink for first class, beige for second, and they hovered around these dingy shades until 1978. On the early tickets there was also a watermark, depicting a ghostly cityscape. The second-class single fare of 15 centimes remained until 1919. Until 1974, the carnet tickets featured a big capital letter that was changed, in alphabetical order, every time a new fare tariff came in, and those letters fix the tickets in history. At the time of the Liberation of Paris in 1944, the tickets bore the letter J. Up until the 1960s, the tickets sometimes bore advertisements on the reverse side, usually for products commensurate with Parisian glamour: women's blouses, liquors, theatres, thermal baths, cat food. Since 1973 there has been a magnetic strip on the reverse side to trigger the automatic barriers. Between 1978 and 1992 tickets were yellow, which contrasted nicely with the brown oxidised strip on the rear which enabled them to be read in ticket barriers. The colours were those of a banana toffee. The RATP certainly seemed to think the yellow was outrageous, hence the slogan *'Ticket chic, ticket choc'*, the latter word meaning 'shock'. This was also the title of a French pop song used to promote the tickets on TV.

From 1992, tickets became jade green, and bore the new RATP logo showing the shape of the River Seine, which *voyageurs* were invited to double-take for an upraised female face in profile. In 2003 tickets became purple, and were actually labelled as 'tickets', the English word, I believe, being applicable to local transport but never to the Grandes Lignes, where tickets are still '*billets*'. Metro tickets have been white since 2007. Since 1968, Metro tickets have also been usable on buses and trams. There are fare zones in the Paris area, but they don't apply to the Metro, so it is a matter of purely academic interest that the Metro lies in zones one, two and three.

Second-class single Metro tickets became less interesting after 1951, when they ceased to show the name of the issuing station. In the superb thriller, *The Wages of Fear*, directed by Henry-Georges Clouzot and released in 1953, four desperadoes living in a remote South American shanty town take on the highly dangerous job of driving two lorry loads of nitroglycerine to an oil well fire. The nitro will (by some method not explained) put out the fire. The motivation of two of them is to make enough money to return to Paris, where they had lived happily. One of them, Mario, has chalked an image of a Guimard entrance on the wall above his bed together with drawings of cavorting naked women. The centrepiece of this display – 'the crown jewels', Mario says – is a Metro ticket in a glass case, and it is more than a souvenir; it is also a token or guarantee that he will return to Paris. It's a second-class ticket with a hole punched in it (so it has been used), and it reads 'Pigalle'. One American film website states that 'Mario treasures a ticket stub from the Paris subway, destination Pigalle.' But Pigalle is the place of origin, not the destination. Metro tickets never stated the destination.

I like Metro tickets because they are very 'tickety', conforming to my ideal. A ticket should be small and hard enough to be lodged in a hat band or used as a toothpick or a roach, or to underline a couple of words, and this ideal of mine is based on the Edmondson tickets used on Britain's railways, even though these were gone by 1990. Metro tickets are 6.5 centimetres by 3cm, which makes them about the same width as an Edmondson, but slightly longer (and 'Ticket de Metro' is the name of the most popular bikini wax among Parisian women).

It is difficult, nonetheless, to argue against the phasing out of Metro tickets, in view of all that wasted paper. The process began in 1975, with the successful introduction of the Carte Orange, a ticket for use in at least two fare zones on all public transport in the Paris area for a week or a month. The Carte reflected the success of the RER, and the fact that it was often used in conjunction with the Metro. In *PARIS RER Handbook*, Brian Patten writes that the seamless-travel principle of the Carte was 'copied by other cities and was the direct inspiration of the London Travelcard'. In 2009, the Carte was replaced by a single Navigo card, which can be linked to the user's account with RATP, so its value need not be lost if it is mislaid or stolen.

But I look warily at the names of the electronic options aimed at the casual visitor to Paris: Navigo Easy and Navigo Liberté. Nothing described as 'Easy' ever is, and as for 'Liberté', what could be freer than a little piece of card allowing its owner to go anywhere in Paris, and completely untraceable to that owner?

The Smell of the Metro

'It's the smell of Paris,' says my Parisian friend Julian Pepinster: 'all the packed-in people and all the good and all the bad.' When the first generation of all-steel Metro trains were stood down in the early 1980s, one ingredient of the Metro's mysterious smell was lost: that of the hot oil on their wooden brake blocks. In *Footprints in Paris: A Few Streets, a Few Lives,* Gillian Tindall describes the smell as 'garlic, dust and tobacco'. Cigarettes were an ingredient until 1991, when smoking on Metro platforms and corridors was banned. It had been legal to smoke on the actual trains (in designated smoking sections) only between 1904 and 1914. The First World War made the Metro overcrowded, and smoking in those conditions was considered dangerous. The French smoke more than the British, and you often see passengers with an unlit cigarette provocatively poised in their lips; it's usually a bluff, but you more often catch a transgressive whiff or wisp of fag smoke on a Metro train than you will on a Tube. The vinegary smell of a slumbering vagrant was more likely to be involved in the days when almost all Metro stations were furnished with those long wooden benches.

I once described the odour as 'lemongrass'; it's possible I was detecting a perfume called Eau de Madeleine, which since 1998 has been added to the wax applied to the bitumen on Metro platforms during nightly cleaning. (The wax is to make the platforms shine, and you can see your blurry reflection in them, as in turbid water.) On 20 April 2001, ABC News described this scent as 'a floral bouquet of rose and jasmine combined with citrus top notes, giving way to strong woody accents and a hint of sweetness in the base'. It might be that people are interested in the Metro aroma because Paris in general is such an odoriferous place, with all its concentrated perfumery, traffic, and outdoor dining. Here is Jean Rhys, from *Quartet*: 'August was a hot, oppressive month, the sun beating down on sleepy streets, the cafés and restaurants nearly empty, the staircase and passages of the Hôtel de Bosphore and its fellows pervaded by an extraordinary mixture of smells ... Drains, face powder, scent, garlic, drains. Above all, drains, Heidler decided.'

When I was writing my column about the London Underground for the London *Evening Standard*, a Swedish man who'd lived briefly in London wrote to me suggesting that the smell of the Underground be bottled and sold to tourists. It was the thing that most typified London, he said, along with the placement of drainpipes on the outsides of buildings. (In Sweden they're inside, so they don't freeze.) But my correspondent didn't attempt to describe the Underground smell, and I've never noticed it. Perhaps this is because you can't smell yourself. I suppose, by the same token, that if I'd been travelling on the Metro every day for decades, I wouldn't be so interested in its fragrance, having become part *of* that whiff.

In *Platform Souls: The Trainspotter as 20th-Century Hero*, Nicholas Whittaker recalls the Metro he found in 1975, when he was in his late teens, to have had a 'bready' smell:

I loved the Metro. The cream and blue carriages had rubber tyres, so things seemed clean and quiet after London's grubby Northern Line. It wasn't just the trains, but the whole ambience: the bready smell, the warning hooters ... What charmed me most were the posters. Instead of far-fetched promises like 'Your firm will love moving to Peterborough ...' there were naked women luxuriating in perfumed soap bubbles. You couldn't smell the lather, yet you knew it was gorgeous and sensual. Even the housewives advertising frozen peas looked chic and sexy. The Paris Metro was an erotic wonderland!

The eroticism of the Metro, incidentally, has been expressed in diverse ways. Condom machines are dotted about the system. In the Forties and Fifties, private detectives advertised on the system, boasting of their ability to catch your spouse in the act of infidelity. On Line 4, in about 1995, a man asked if he could borrow my pen, so he could write a woman's phone number on the back of a Metro ticket, which is one benefit of passengers being able to retain the ticket after the journey. I'm not sure if the woman gave him the right number, because after he alighted, she began joking with her friend about him. My French wasn't up to a full translation, but the woman was shaking her head and said 'Incroyable' twice, and it wasn't the good sort of incredible.

Tuileries on Line 1, being one of the special, themed stations, has a display about important moments during the Metro's first century, and these include the birth of Brigitte Bardot, who is pictured. Also pictured is Josephine Baker, who is shown topless, which she wouldn't be on the London Underground. And the code governing Metro advertisements is certainly more permissive than the Underground's. On a Line 2 train a couple of years ago, I saw an advertisement for some mysterious object promoted as *'Womaniser Passage du Désir Cadeaux'*. When I googled this, I got a warning of explicit content: it was a vibrator. Towards Christmas 2022, I saw an advert on a Line 12 station for a 'Naughty and Nice' advent calendar, the advert placed by adameteve.fr (*'Site de jouets pour adultes'*).

V

PORTRAITS OF THE LINES

Line 1

The best way to appreciate the growth of the Metro is to watch an animation on YouTube called 'Paris Metro Expansion 1900–2030', which shows the development of the lines against a background of soothing elevator-type music. It's from the site of Ashley Rabot ('a town planner by day and transport fanatic at night'). Even though the animated lines appear to slither quickly across the city, the film lasts 24 minutes, a reflection of the density of the Metro and its restlessness. I do not propose to track quite every inch of Metro growth – that would be unreadable – but what follows is a sketch of the development of each line, with a magnifying glass applied to moments, or scenes, of particular interest. I will take the lines in numerical order, which is not quite the same as their chronological order, but Line 1 really was the first.

It was opened at 1 p.m. on 19 July 1900, a couple of months after the opening of the Paris Exposition, but that was no big deal – the line was merely fashionably late, given that the Exposition would continue until November. It ran from Porte Maillot in the west to Porte de Vincennes in the east, paralleling the course of the river in the centre and following the transverse axis of the Grande Croisée beneath the Champs-Élysées

and rue de Rivoli. It also connected those two forests, Bois de
Boulogne to the west and Bois de Vincennes to the east, which
Paris wears like big green earmuffs. Initially, eight stations
were opened; by the year's end there were eighteen.

As mentioned, several of the stations (Concorde, Palais
Royal-Musée du Louvre, Gare de Lyon) have flat roofs reinforced by great girders – *tablier métallique*, rather than flowing
arches. This permits a shallower excavation, necessitated on
riverside Line 1 by the need to clear the water table. Another
reason is that this kind of excavation is quicker than vault-
creation, and Bienvenüe was up against a tight deadline here,
what with the imminence of the 1900 Expo. *Tablier métallique*
is less aesthetic than vault-creation, but more expensive, and
so we can regard those great riveted iron beams as so much
overhead bling – Bienvenüe throwing money at a problem.

The line does break the surface at Bastille. The *voyageur*
knows something dramatic is about to happen, because the line
enters the sharpest curve on the Metro; then suddenly ... sky,
treetops and the Canal St Martin glittering away to the right
on its course towards the river. The Line 1 Bastille station is
actually on a bridge over the canal, and so is very intimate with
it. The curve, by the way, is caused by the line's straining in a
southward direction to connect with Gare de Lyon.

Gare de Lyon main-line station was unusual in being served
by only one Metro line until 1998, when Line 14 went there.
It has never been one of the big commuter stations, having its
mind on higher things, like the Riviera, destination of many of
its trains. A significant percentage of its users have been too

rich to bother with the Metro, including the British heading for the southbound *trains de luxe*. The present Gare de Lyon is the third station to occupy the site, and the clocktower of the present one, opened for the Exposition in 1900, suggests a more florid Big Ben, in acknowledgement of *le trafic anglais.*

I've spent a lot of time hanging around Gare de Lyon, looking at rail-related sites while waiting for trains. It's worth de-training from the Metro to look at another. Running east to west just north of the station, along Avenue Daumesnil, is the Viaduc des Arts, which looks as if it should be carrying a railway line, instead of what is actually up there: a pleasant linear garden and walkway (with shops, workshops and cafés in the arches below). Of course, it did once carry a railway: the line from Vincennes in east Paris to Gare de la Bastille, the smallest Parisian terminus, which was at its busiest in the 1930s. Its operations were pretty exotic. Commuters came in by double-decker steam trains, and 'freight' seems too crude a word for the cargoes brought to Bastille, such as wine from the Marne valley vineyards, and flowers. In summer 1897 a nocturnal Train des Roses carried a million blooms every night to the Gare de la Bastille. The station was demolished in 1984. Today the Bastille Opera House (which Richard Cobb hated) occupies the site, and commuters from the territory served by the railway now use RER Line A.

I often go to Le Train Bleu, the opulent restaurant located at the top of an operatic double staircase in Gare de Lyon and decorated with frescoes of the South of France, but never for a full meal, since even the express 'Menu Voyageur' is fifty quid a head. I might run to a *demi bier* and a bowl of nuts in the drinking lounge off the main area, which I preferred in the days when it was screened off by purple velvet curtains, and the Train Bleu black cat prowled around.

In *Parisians: An Adventure History of Paris*, Graham Robb gives a vivid evocation of Line 1 on opening day. *Voyageurs* buy their tickets – 'rectangles of pink or cream card, with a background design that might have been a cathedral or a power station'. On the platform, they encounter a 'stench of creosote' and 'the aquarium light of electric lamps'. (The sleepers of the Metro tracks used to be seasoned with creosote – a practice curtailed because it caused breathing difficulties for some passengers.) A train draws in: 'three wooden crates'. The *voyageurs* board, encountering 'fluted wood furniture and polished wooden decking'. As the train moves off, it throws up 'huge blue sparks leaping through the darkness like ghostly dolphins escorting a ship'.

There's still a sense of primacy about Line 1, of smugness, almost. It connects a lot of grandeur: Arc de Triomphe (served by Charles de Gaulle Étoile station), Tuileries, Louvre etc. It's the busiest line, and the sleekest, with the newest trains anywhere to be seen on the network (outside the freakishly futuristic Line 14): the driverless MP05s. The walk-through carriages feature the chicest seat moquettes, or seat coverings, on the Metro: broad stripes in warm reds, greens and purples – striking, Fauvist colours that demand your attention. And these

trains convey the smartest *voyageurs*, whether they be cultur-
ally attuned tourists en route to the Louvre, or the business folk
of La Défense. The children who sit at the front pretending to
drive the train are applauded by their well-coiffured mothers:
'Bravo, Pierre!' as the cossetted *garçon* executes another inch-
perfect station stop. The line colour, officially described as
'buttercup', is jolly and optimistic. Line 1 seems to be perpetu-
ating the boasting of the 1900 Exposition.

The star of the previous Exposition, in 1889, had been a
static phenomenon: the Eiffel Tower, which was modern by
virtue of its great height, but not at all electrified. Even its
lifts were hydraulic. The 1900 Exposition, by contrast, was all
about movement and electricity: a moving walkway, elevators,
the new Metro – which served the main Expo sights on the
Right Bank, including Trocadéro and the Grand Palais and
the Petit Palais, both accessible from Marbeuf station, now
called Franklin D. Roosevelt. Those Beaux-Arts *palais* resemble monumental railway stations, and another new building,
opened in 1900 and lying a little further east on the opposite
bank, actually was a railway station: Gare d'Orsay, which only
operated until 1939, becoming thereafter a great, haunted
house in the middle of Paris, occasionally used as a film set,
for instance by Orson Welles for his film of Kafka's novel,
The Trial, or by Bertolucci for *The Conformist*. In *Nairn's Paris*
(1968), Ian Nairn described it as 'a great curved shell with the
scale of St Pancras – filled now with railway junk, parked cars
and a few wee lines that peter off miserably to the *banlieue* from
a lower level'.

When the station opened in 1900, the painter Édouard Detaille called it 'superb' and said it 'looks like an art gallery'. It became one in 1986, when it was opened as the Musée d'Orsay – later than I thought when I was writing a novel partly set in the Paris of the 1970s. I had one of the principal characters visiting the Musée d'Orsay; a reader pointed out the mistake, politely enough.

There was a poetic justice in this, because for years, I have enjoyed challenging, and irritating, my fellow English in Paris by pointing to the Musée d'Orsay and asking, as a preliminary question: 'I assume you know this used to be a railway station?' They usually do know. (A clue is in the giant gilded clock that frowns down at you as you view the exhibits.) I then ask, 'How do you think the trains got in?' since, after all, the river lies directly in front of the building, which is hemmed in by other buildings – all of which have obviously been there for a long time – on the other three sides. The answer is that the trains arrived and departed by subterranean lines running beneath the Left Bank of the river to Gare d'Austerlitz to the east. The Paris-Orléans company, proprietors of Gare d'Austerlitz, wanted to project their service into the middle of town, so they built Orsay as a head station. There was never a Metro station to serve Gare d'Orsay, but it was itself a Metro-like station, being subterranean, electrified (passengers descended towards the electric trains in electric lifts, while their luggage was carried down on electric conveyor belts), and centrally located – and today its undercroft where the trains themselves ran has been revived as the Musée D'Orsay station of RER Line C.

We have noted that Fulgence Bienvenüe favoured simple, straight up-and-down lines in principle, so it's irritating to have to mention that in 1900 Line 1 featured two branches, both served by shuttles. The first ran south-west from Étoile to Porte Dauphine, handy for the Bois de Boulogne, and the CMP anticipated that plenty of visitors to the Expo would want to repair to the woods as an escape from the tense hum of all that electricity. The second branch also ran from Étoile, but in a more directly southerly direction – to Trocadéro, where many of the Expo pavilions congregated. The first branch would be given to Line 2, the second to Line 6, and we are unfortunately in for a lot of this shuffling about of lines and stations. We should note another operational feature of Line 1, and this would become common to many Metro lines. There were tight track loops at the termini – Porte de Vincennes and Porte Maillot – to avoid the need for trains to reverse.

Line 1 was helped by the fact that it opened in a heatwave. Parisians discovered the truth of a slogan sometimes used in the 1920s to advertise London Underground – 'It's cooler down below' – and still used to advertise the Paris Catacombs. It took half an hour to cross Paris using the line, a trip that had taken about three hours by horse-drawn bus. At first the trains had a frequency of every ten minutes – 'perhaps similar to an evening service in August today', writes Clive Lamming in *The Story of the Paris Metro*, which reminds us that the Metro, unlike the London Underground, is seasonal: fewer trains run in August because so many Parisians leave the city in that month. (The trains removed from service are stashed away all over the system, often in the terminal loops, where they are preyed on by graffiti artists, all of whom seem to stay in Paris during August for the easy pickings.)

The frequency was soon increased to every six minutes during rush hours, and it was every three at the beginning of 1901 – modifications attesting to the great success of the line. In 1900 Line 1 carried 18 million people; in 1903 the Metro was carrying 100 million; in 1917, 500 million; in 1943, as we have seen, over a billion. The figure hovered between 1 and 1.2 billion in the second half of the twentieth century, but there has been a major increase since. In 2018, 1.56 billion were carried. London Underground did not reach a billion until 2007.

In 1934, the year the Metro began probing beyond the city boundaries, Line 1 was extended east from Porte de Vincennes to Château de Vincennes, which required the loop at Porte de Vincennes to be dismantled. In 1937, Line 1 was extended west from Porte Maillot to Pont de Neuilly, the new tracks going underneath the loop. That's the trouble with loops: they get in the way when you want to extend, which the Metro often does. In 1992, Line 1 was extended further west to La Défense, where, incidentally, it awaits Line 15 of the Grand Paris Express. The extension meant that Line 1 had to cross the Seine, which might surprise some tourists, who probably think – I know I did – that, having mooched through central Paris, the Seine was done with the city; they don't realise that it writhes in such a way that it recurs immediately west of Paris. Line 1 crosses the river in Metro-dramatic circumstances: by climbing sharply up to a bridge it shares with the Route

Nationale 14. But that's nothing compared to the line that really pioneered Metro-drama: Line 2.

Line 2

You don't have to be on Line 2 to see it, because it is elevated (Metro Aérien) in its central section, where it crosses the gaping steel maws of Gare du Nord and Gare de l'Est main-line stations.

Much of Line 6 is also elevated, and it can be considered the South Bank counterpart of Line 2. The lines form two semi-circles, with Line 2 at the top, Line 6 at the bottom. Since the elevated parts of Line 2 run through working-class areas, whereas those of Line 6 run through prosperous ones, I think of Line 2 Metro Aérien as a frown and Line 6 Metro Aérien as a smile. Both are beautiful, though.

It is between Barbes Rochechouart and La Chapelle stations that the Line 2 viaduct, running along boulevard de la Chapelle, passes over the Gare du Nord lines. The view of the massed and jumbled tracks is spectacular in heavy rain or at night, both of which suit Gare du Nord, when the red, green and amber signal lamps resemble so many blurred jewels; and immediately afterwards, you see another array of Grandes Lignes – those coming out of Gare de l'Est. In each case, you are experiencing Metro-drama as well as a kind of timeslip, back to the days when railways ruled the world, and it is hard to believe that anyone alive today understands the purpose of all those lines.

'Gare du Nord', an essay of 1986 by Jacques Reda, collected in a volume called *Paris Metro Tales*, contains the following passage: 'From La Chapelle the overground metro affords a terrifying view of the exit, where, like surgeons' knives in a wide open-open black bag, the rails shine at night under the ghostly glow of Sacré-Coeur, under the last splashes of the long pornographic meat-factory that gapes near Barbès.'

There is something baleful about Gare du Nord; it's rather factory-like itself. 'In the morning, the first night trains, arriving from Belgium and Germany, bring the first load of crooks,' wrote George Simenon in *Maigret's Memoirs*, 'with faces as hard as the light that falls through the window panes.'

I always congratulate myself if I am on Line 2 looking down at Gare du Nord in the evening rather than being *in* Gare du Nord and looking up at it, because this means I have another night in Paris ahead of me. And I stress that I am not necessarily heading for Pigalle, the first subterranean station west of the Line 2 viaduct. (In Richard Cobb mode, I can remember the days when, if you got out at Pigalle and walked along boulevard de Clichy to re-join Line 2 at Blanche, you passed 500 metres of blazing sex shop neon. It's toned down now, the shops selling things slightly less readily available on the Internet than pornography, like rubber gear and sex toys.)

Three stops further west after Pigalle comes Rome station, and between here and the next stop west, Villiers, is another outbreak of Metro-drama, but you must get off the train to see it. This is where Line 2 crosses over the railway canyon at Batignolles, formed in 1912 when the roof of a giant tunnel was removed. Line 2, being underground at this point, achieves the crossing by running in a tunnel attached to the underneath of a bridge carrying a road over the canyon. From the train you can't tell you're in this tunnel, but the *tablier métallique* at Rome station, signifying closeness to the surface, gives a clue that something is up.

Alight at Rome to examine this monstrous set-up. You can't miss the Batignolles trench, where the trains rattle into and out of Gare Saint-Lazare. 'Paris Saint-Lazare' is written on the cutting wall in enormous letters, white on red, like licensed graffiti. Perched atop the cutting on the west side stands what appears to be an old Wagons-Lits restaurant car, but is actually a restaurant called Le Wagon Bleu. It looks grotty in daylight but, illuminated in blue and gold on a rainy night, it's alluring. I've eaten there several times; the cuisine is Corsican, therefore not quite commensurate with Wagons-Lits cordon bleu, but very good. The 'carriage' is actually mocked up using parts from Wagons-Lits day cars, but it does have the silk-shaded table lamps associated with the CIWL, whose sybaritic spirit is honoured by a blackboard in the attached cocktail bar that boasts seventy-five beers and sixty wines.

A little way south is the Pont de L'Europe, a vantage point for admirers of expressed infrastructure, since it overlooks both the canyon and the tracks into Gare Saint-Lazare, used by main-line trains in from Normandy and the local services dubbed 'Translien'. This very scene, albeit with steam trains, was evoked by Zola in *La Bête humaine*, and painted by Edouard Manet, Claude Monet and Gustave Caillebotte, all following

Zola's injunction to 'find the poetry of stations as [our] fathers found that of forests and rivers'. Zola died in 1902 (possibly murdered for his support of Dreyfus), so he had two years to observe the Metro. I don't think he ever wrote about it, but he is commemorated by Avenue Émile Zola Metro station on Line 10.

The original plan for the Metro included a circular route, following the wide boulevards that had replaced the old wall of the Farmers General. In the event, the two separate half circles would be built, meeting at Étoile to the west and Nation to the east. You would never be able to run around the circle on a single train; you would always have to change at either Étoile or Nation. The northern half of the circle was originally called Line 2 North, the other Line 2 South. Line 2 North became just plain Line 2; Line 2 South would eventually become Line 6.

The main part of Line 2 was opened in 1903. The line was also given the spur between Étoile and Porte Dauphine that had originally belonged to Line 1. This was a prestigious addition, connecting two posh locations, but it was untidy, in that it lay beyond the circular double act formed by Line 2 North and Line 2 South. (Diagrammatically, we can think of that spur as being the very short tail of a very fat and round pig.)

The two lines are elevated for a variety of reasons. Line 6 would have to cross the Seine, and a less well-known, hidden river, the Bièvre (which is currently being exhumed and rehabilitated). Line 2 would have to cross, besides the Gare du Nord and Gare de l'Est lines, those of the Gare Saint-Lazare, and the Canal St Martin. The boulevards along which the two lines ran were wide enough to accommodate viaducts, so in that sense their generous scale was their undoing. Line 2 has four elevated stations, Line 6 thirteen (almost half the line), but *voyageurs'* impressions of the two will tend to blur into one.

The elevated sections of both were built by the same pair: Louis Biette (engineer), and Jean-Camille Formigé (designer – who also designed the Columbarium at Père Lachaise and the garden in front of Sacré-Coeur). The tracks run over a series of truss bridges, and it's as if a very enthusiastic kid had been given a rogue Meccano set comprising only truss bridge components. The bridges are supported on Corinthian steel columns, with stone piers helping out when it comes to the stations and intermittently elsewhere. I am reminded of the seaside: the stone buttresses are like sea walls; the columns like the legs of a pier, and the successive curves of the truss bridge tops are wave-like. In both cases, the viaducts are prettified in a gauche but charming way. The columns are painted silver, and there are decorative motifs on the masonry: wreaths, cornucopia and the Paris coat of arms, which is a ship, in acknowledgement of its Roman origins as a trading place on the island of the Seine, but the ship looks to be on the sea, and the motto, *Fluctuat nec Mergitur* ('It is tossed by the waves but does not sink'), also suggests the sea. This blazon used to appear, painted in gold leaf, on the sides of the Sprague cars, and its use in this way chimes in my mind with the use of *'voyageur'* to describe passengers.

Both lines cover a wide social range, but I always thought of

Line 6 as the more salubrious. In the first place, it is the more literally uplifting because it has more elevated stations, and its elevated sections lie mainly in the upmarket 15th and 16th Arrondissements, where it traverses the river alongside the Eiffel Tower on the beautiful Pont de Bir-Hakeim.

The elevated part of Line 2, on the other hand, cuts through the 10th Arrondissement where, as Stephen Clarke writes in *Paris Revealed: The Secret Life of a City*, it 'gives views into some of the poorest apartments in Paris'. This is the area due north of Gare du Nord, which, in *A Moveable Feast*, Hemingway called the 'dirtiest and saddest part of town'. Today, it is home to African and Sri Lankan immigrants, and I would call it neither dirty nor sad, although there is a refugee camp underneath the Line 2 viaduct between Barbes Rochechouart and La Chapelle. (The viaducts of both 2 and 6 provide roofs over the boulevards, and rough sleepers, and the organisers of fairs and markets, have always taken advantage.)

There is more graffiti on the stone and steel of the Line 2 viaducts, but the stations on Line 2 are arguably more attractive: they have ornate canopies (like an English country station), rather than the glass roofs of Line 6; and Line 2 stations have glass walls, and so are lighter than those on Line 6, which have brick walls. At Jaurès on Line 2, creepers of (I think plastic) ivy hang from the canopy, and at the start of the film *Subway*, when a posh looking, dinner-jacketed Christophe Lambert makes his initial dive into the Metro where he will be spending most of the film, he is riding a Line 2 train as it descends from its viaduct, not a Line 6.

In both cases, you seem to be floating through Paris, partly owing to the quietness of the trains. The Line 6 ones, dating from 1973, are quiet because they have tyres, hence the designation MP73. It was the priority at the time to spare the genteel inhabitants of the adjacent blocks the infernal clattering that their predecessors – or the same people when younger – were subject to in the days of the resonant Sprague stock. Line 2 has more modern trains, MF01s, which do have steel wheels but are engineered to be quiet.

A word about the MF01s, which are also on Lines 5 and 9. They have huge windows, and their internal colour schemes refute the chilliness and insipidity of the grey and light blue tones used in so many modern train interiors. The MF01s are cosy, with illuminated line diagrams above the door set into glass panels of midnight blue. The bulkheads between passenger accommodation and driver's cab are painted maroon, an old-fashioned railway colour that adds to the cosiness, as do the greens, reds and oranges of the narrow stripes (like Paul Smith's signature stripes) of the moquette used on these trains.

The narrow stripes of this moquette, along with the broad, bold stripes on the MP05s, we described as Fauvist – the best designs on the network. They are RATP designs but, as a Yorkshireman, I'm pleased to say they were developed for production twenty years ago by the Yorkshire moquette-making firm of Holdsworth and Co., and were then manufactured by another Yorkshire firm, Camira, which by then had acquired Holdsworth. These two designs were prepared for the loom at Holdsworth by David Hallgarth and his staff, and David spoke to me by phone from his home in Hebden Bridge, Yorkshire. (I mention that just to get Hebden Bridge into a book about the Paris Metro.)

'I thought the designs were splendid,' David told me. 'Some of the colours used were long established – a classic green, for instance.' They reminded him of some of the highly regarded interwar moquette designs for London Underground produced by Enid Marx and Marion Dorn, among others, and I would indeed rate those two moquettes as more attractive than any currently on London Underground. But generally, the Underground has better seats than the Metro. It always uses true moquette, which has a high percentage of wool and a thick pile, whereas some Metro lines have seats covered in a thinnish, worn, man-made fibre of an undistinguished shade. See for instance the blue-fading-to-grey on the Line 12 MF67s. Such is the relaxed mood created by the mellow colours of the Line 2 MF01s that I always expect to sink comfortably into their seats. They are rock hard, however. Hard seats – wood, in the case of the Spragues – have long been the Metro norm. London Underground seats, on the other hand, used to be soft. A curator at the London Transport Museum told me that punters quite often fall asleep in the 1938 Tube Stock carriage on display, so comfy are the seats. But London Underground train seats have been getting harder ever since steel springs were removed from the upholstery, so one of those 'cultural differences' between the two systems is fading. The Metro was conceived of as tram-like, offering short rides across a relatively small city. The Underground traversed longer distances, and the English are more domesticated than the French, more attached to home and hearth, so for many years they were given, in effect, armchairs on their trains.

We ourselves now return to Line 2 as it continues west towards Porte Dauphine. You get a different class of *voyageurs* on this stretch: trim, cat-like women and sleek-looking men in those shortie macs the French favour. Anywhere west of Pigalle, you probably won't be warned by a stranger to guard your mobile phone from pickpockets, as I once was further east on the line.

The smarter sections of the Metro, such as this one, attract the most buskers. Busking on Metro trains, as opposed to in designated parts of station corridors (where whole mini orchestras of East Europeans can be heard) is prohibited, but it's often done – an instance of that familiar French one-two: make a strict rule, then tolerate its infringement, hence the relaxedness about those who circumvent the ticket barriers. My friend the railway consultant maintains that this is the French approach to European Community rules, and that if Britain had been equally cynical, or worldly, about them, Brexit need never have happened.

The typical Metro on-train busker is a hangdog old man playing a wheezy accordion or perhaps a battered Spanish guitar with a pick-up held on by Sellotape. 'They're usually pickpockets as well,' says my Francophobe friend, but when I asked how they combined this with the musicianship, he changed the subject: 'Isn't it your round?' Since the on-train busker is itinerant, he carries his amplifier on a little trolley, like a shopping bag on wheels, which adds to the sense of decrepitude. He is a like a ghost from the past, trying to make himself noticed in carriages full of phone callers or Internet browsers, the signal on the Metro being much more consistent than on the London Underground, which is which riddled with 'not-spots'.

On 28 July 2016, Elijah Wald, musician and author, posted on his website (elijahwald.com) a memory of Paris in the late 1970s, in which he describes a bar called Le Mazet on the rue Saint André des Arts and 'down a passageway from the Odéon Metro station' as 'the buskers' bar'.

'It was populated by male musicians from various countries and teenage French girls who worked as "bottlers" [money collectors],' he writes. 'The musicians were basically lazy and would play the trains for a couple of hours, then come back to the Mazet, change their bills into coins and have a few beers.'

Le Mazet is still extant and has live music on some nights. It is rumoured that Jim Morrison had the last of his many drinks there. Another rock rumour is that Mick Jagger discovered Sugar Blue, who played the brilliant harmonica solo on the Stones' song 'Miss You', when he (Sugar Blue, of course) was busking on the Metro. But this would have required Mick Jagger to be *on* the Metro, and I don't see that happening, even though he does sometimes live in Paris.

At the Porte Dauphine terminus stands that surviving Guimard *édicule* – the pot of gold at the end of the rainbow. There is also a tight loop of track – a terminal loop of the kind

PORTRAITS OF THE LINES 155

that often featured on the early Metro, and I feel that Metro
loops justify the digression that follows. Not all readers might
agree, in which case they are encouraged to skip the next few
paragraphs.

The trains at Porte Dauphine enter the loop after (theoreti-
cally) shedding their passengers. They either park in the loop
(if they're going out of service) or run around it, returning to
a platform adjacent to the one they occupied before entering
the loop and now facing the right direction for the return trip.
Voyageurs are supposed to get off the train before it goes into the
loop, but this process of 'tipping out' passengers, as it's called in
London, might be quite cursory – all part of the casualness of
the system: the assumption that you will have the savoir-faire
to co-exist with the unequivocal diktats: 'Défense de Fumer et
de Cracher', and so on.

I'm sure many tourists have been carried into terminal loops,
not noticing the subtle signals: that they'd reached the end of
the line; that all the other passengers had vacated the platforms;
that the electronic indicator on the platform had gone blank.

The terminal loops of Line 1 may have been overridden by
line extensions but, aside from Porte Dauphine, they remain
at Porte des Lilas on *3bis* and at Porte de Clignancourt on
Line 4. There is only one loop of this kind on the London
Underground – at Kennington on the Northern Line. Rail
enthusiasts and thrill seekers (the categories are not mutu-
ally exclusive) try to dodge the driver when he 'tips out' at

Kennington to experience the carousel-ride of this loop. They can then order a T-shirt reading 'I've ridden the Kennington Loop', and I have often thought that the wearing of such an item might be a very quick way of committing social suicide.

The goal of the type of railway enthusiast called a 'track basher' is to travel over as much track as possible, and to ride over a stretch of line not normally accessible to the public. It's the kind of thing these people dine out on. (Not that they ever do dine out.) Whether they would be equally interested to learn that the Metro also has terminal loops for passengers *and* trains is moot, because this is licensed loop riding: anyone can do it. In these cases, the station is located on a loop in such a way that, whether arriving or departing, you see half the loop, and if arriving *and* departing (i.e. staying on the train, as a rail enthusiast might), you'd see all of it, and it does look interesting – not quite intended for public scrutiny, like the backstage of a theatre.

A terminal loop of any sort is surely more entertaining than the usual London arrangement: the train remains on the terminal platform while the driver plods from one end to the other. If the train is about be taken into a siding and out of service, he checks the carriages, perhaps waking any sleepers by banging his cab door key on a hand rail, but if the train is scheduled to go back down the line he doesn't bother about anyone who has remained on the train, and he avoids eye contact with anyone poised to *board* the train just in case they should ask him a question. At either end of the train, he might pause to unlock a small cupboard in the platform wall, where a hot water tap is secreted (a 'tea point'), where he might replenish his billy can.

Actually, I suppose that is all quite interesting in a gnomic way, but I enjoy riding around track loops: it makes a change from going in a straight line, which is what trains usually do. There's something enjoyably daft about ending up where you started from, and there's a commensurately oxymoronic term for it: looping the loop. If we jump to the other terminus of Line 2, at Nation, we will encounter one of these passenger-carrying loops.

Whether you are entering or leaving Nation on Line 2 by this loop, it feels as if the train has lost its way, as it rumbles past sidings on which stand empty, parked MF01s, with technical hieroglyphs on the tunnel walls. Line 2 shares Nation with Lines 1 and 9, and RER Line A, and this railway complex lies beneath a great, baleful traffic roundabout with a monument to liberty – Triumph of the Republic – in the centre. The name Nation was given on Bastille Day 1880. During the Revolution it had been called Place du Trône Renversé (Square of the Toppled Throne), and guillotines were set up here. I did once ascend to the surface at Nation. Any given square or roundabout in Paris is likely to have a Metro loop beneath it (there being no house basements in the way), and the subterranean goings-on at Nation are certainly more interesting than those on the surface.

Line 6 also has passenger-carrying terminal loops at Nation and Étoile; and there's one at Place d'Italie on Line 5. Besides the train-only loops and the passenger-carrying ones, there's

a third category of loop on the Metro, and these are visible
on the map; they corral several stations, and we will come to
them when we discuss the lines on which they occur: 7*bis* and
10. There are similar big loops on London Underground, at
Heathrow and on the eastern end of the Central Line, but the
consultant railway engineer I know said he considered the
Metro's enthusiasm for loops of various kinds to be nothing less
than 'the biggest cultural difference between the two systems',
and that Loopism is deeply engrained in the Metro: 'The trains
have shorter carriages than London Underground trains, so
they curve through a tighter radius. And that continued to be
true even when they built trains with walk-through carriages.'

When I asked him to explain the Parisian preference
for loops, he fell silent for a while. 'Are they quicker?' I
prompted him.

'... Maybe,' he said, after a long pause. 'What they definitely
are,' he said, after another pause, 'is simpler.'

'You mean more elegant?'

This time his answer was prompt.

'Yes.'

In comparing lines 2 and 6, I have implied a certain melancholy
about the former. This might be traced back to 1903.

At seven o'clock on 10 August, smouldering was discovered on a train at Barbès station, which is an elevated station,
now called Barbès Rochechouart. The carriages were mainly
wooden, as with all Metro trains of the time. The passengers

were evacuated from the train, and from the next one that came into the station, and this second one was used to push the first eastwards along the line towards Belleville, where there was an underground siding in which it might be safely parked while the fire was dealt with – all of which seems bizarre, because surely a burning train ought to be kept in the open air? It turned out that the points were not set for the Belleville siding, so the convoy, now trailing thick black smoke, continued towards the easterly terminus of Line 2, at Nation.

But the convoy didn't get as far as Nation. At Ménilmontant, two stops beyond Belleville, a full fire broke out. Meanwhile, another train had forsaken the open air and entered the tunnel; this one was packed with *voyageurs* – all the people who'd been turfed off the burning train and its successor. When this crowded train reached Couronnes, the station before Ménilmontant, the station master ordered all the passengers off, and out of the station, in view of what was happening up ahead. But the irate *voyageurs* refused to leave, or not without a refund on their tickets, and they set up a chant of '*Nos trois sous*', a reference to the second-class flat fare, three-twentieths of a franc or fifteen centimes, which was not a lot even in those days. They were then overwhelmed with black smoke blown back from Ménilmonant. Eighty-four people died of carbon monoxide poisoning. 'It was a tragedy of overwhelming proportions,' writes Tamara Hovey in *Paris Underground*, 'and a mood of mourning seized the nation. Telegrams of condolence poured in from all over the world. A solemn mass was performed at the Cathedral Notre Dame ... In the two weeks following the tragedy, the average number of travellers on the Metro fell by half.'

Across the Channel, Tovey adds, 'terrified Londoners deserted the Tube for buses'. Yet today there is no commemoration of this accident at Couronnes, whereas the 1987 King's Cross fire on the London Underground, in which thirty-one people died, is commemorated in the King's Cross ticket hall with a plaque. The lack of a memorial at Couronnes is surprising, given Paris's absorption in its own history. Perhaps it is felt that present-day *voyageurs* would be discouraged by being reminded of the disaster.

It would, however, change the Metro. The two motor cars of the train, which were at either end (the other six cars being so-called trailer cars, with no motors), had been connected by a 600-volt cable; a short circuit here had been the source of the fire. Those first-generation trains would be replaced by the Sprague stock: multiple-unit trains made of steel rather than wood, in which power and traction controls were more safely distributed along the length of the train, although wooden trailer cars continued to run on the elevated lines, where the danger of fire was supposed to be less (Couronnes notwithstanding), until the early 1930s. Henceforth all stations would have fire alarms and hydrants, easier means of escape from below-ground areas; exits and track tunnels would be better illuminated, with good old paraffin lamps. Electricity had shown that it could bite; the triumphalism of the 1900 Exposition was temporarily refuted.

Line 3

Line 3, which opened in 1904, runs east–west through the North Bank, roughly paralleling Line 1, but in less glamorous circumstances. The interest, for the casual *voyageur*, lies to the north-east where, in 1921, the Line had reached Porte des Lilas, having been extended from its original terminus at Gambetta. Porte des Lilas has little of the beauty suggested by its name, but does have some of the tranquillity, being a quiet part of town.

In 1971, the line was extended directly east from Gambetta to Gallieni, to serve a large new bus interchange and housing development, and the quiet stretch running north-east to Lilas suffered a demotion, becoming a self-contained branch, labelled *3bis*.

Line *3bis*, whose official colour is periwinkle, is an endearing runt. There is a railway connection at Gambetta between it and Line 3 proper, but it is seldom used, and *3bis* is a world of its own. Its southern terminus at Gambetta is a rare dead-end (no loops or sidings); at the other end, Porte des Lilas, there is a terminal loop. Line *3bis* is the shortest and least used line, being just ahead of – or behind – *7bis* in this respect. A journey along it takes four minutes. The trains are also short, and old: the MF67s in three-car formation. (Sprague stock trains lingered here until 1981.)

The *3bis* stations (all underground, like those of Line 3 proper) are usually almost deserted, and there are no announcements on the trains. In *The Story of the Paris Metro*, Clive Lamming speaks of a 'strange labyrinth of Metros' up there in the hills of north-eastern Paris, where Lines 3, 7 and 11 cohabit, with their unusually deep, peaceful stations, unfrequented by tourists, and there is something poignant about Porte des Lilas.

I first went there one rainy evening in 2001 and, for some reason I can't remember, I walked. The district around the station was dour: a prison-like army barracks, a perfunctory children's park, a slip road for the Périphérique. The Metro station has a surface building, designed by Charles Plumet, and it struck me as the aesthetic highlight of the district. The style of Plumet (who did the other two stations on *3bis*) might be called functional Art Nouveau, and Porte des Lilas station is mainly of concrete and cement, and badly scarred by graffiti, but it is subtly exotic, with a scalloped roof reminiscent of a seaside pavilion. Delicate little mosaics are set into the walls.

I was due to attend a nocturnal Metro tour, run by ADEMAS (Association d'Exploitation du Matériel Sprague), the organisation founded by my friend Julian Pepinster. The rendezvous was for 11.45 on the '*quai mort*', or dead platform, at Lilas. Since it was not yet eleven, I walked into the bar over the road, which seemed the only other illuminated building in Porte des Lilas. At the appointed time, I crossed the road, and was at first perplexed as to how to enter the station. Then I realised I had to do something not usually required of a Metro *voyageur*: call a lift. (It's the need to house lift gear that explains those *3bis* surface buildings.)

The *quai mort* turned out to be two platforms under a vaulted ceiling in the usual Metro style. It is quite separate from the 'live' platforms at the station that are still in use and serving lines *3bis* and 11. Back in 1921, the purpose of the *quai mort* was to allow Porte des Lilas to receive an extension to Line 7. We have not yet reached Line 7 in our survey, but let us anticipate and say that it opened in 1910, with two branches serving north-east Paris. One of those branches terminated in a large loop serving three stations, because the CMP hadn't been able to decide which of them should be the terminus. The most easterly station on that loop was, and is, Pré-Saint-Gervais. The *quai mort* at Lilas was intended to serve the tracks in two tunnels connecting to that loop, but the CMP decided it wouldn't be worth making a full connection, so a mere shuttle service called the Navette ran back and forth to Pré-Saint-Gervais on one of the two tunnels. The shuttle was never very busy, and it was killed off at the outbreak of war, hence *'quai mort'*.

But there is another, more cheerful, name for *quai mort*, and that is 'Porte des Lilas Cinéma', because film scenes are shot here, in what is effectively a museum. The two platforms are perfectly preserved in the old CMP style, and it's as if a green Sprague stock train has clattered through a minute beforehand. There's a white-tiled booth projecting from the white tiles of the station wall, which would have housed the station manager. All stations used to have these, and a few remain on 'live' parts of the network: there's one at Pernety on Line 13, for example

(it's used as a showcase for art by a local school), and one at
Sèvres Babylone on Line 12. Lilas also retains the primitive,
collapsible wooden seats at the platform entrances, where the
poinçonneuse or *poinçonneur* would have sat while glumly, if
Serge Gainsbourg's song, evoking this very station, is anything
to go by, punching the tickets. There are also the old-fashioned
long benches. Where the station name should be written in tiles
on the platform walls, there are blanks, so the film-makers can
call it what they like. The names they choose usually reflect
a conventional view of Metro glamour, so they pick centrally
located stations. I don't think Porte des Lilas is often called
Porte des Lilas in the films shot there – another aspect of its
poignancy. The films include *Amélie*, in which Lilas masquer-
ades as Abbesses, and *Paris, Je T'aime*, a portmanteau film by
various directors, including the Coen Brothers, who disguised
Lilas as Tuileries to shoot their contribution, a violent little tale
in which Steve Buscemi, playing an innocent tourist, becomes
embroiled with a couple rowing on the opposite platform.

Oddly enough, though, Porte des Lilas *is* called Porte des
Lilas in the film *Julie and Julia*, in which it is represented as
being the home station of the gauche American cookery writer,
Julia Child. Child, who was married to an American diplo-
mat, did live in Paris, but on de rue de l'Université in the 7th,
nowhere near Porte des Lilas. Perhaps the film-makers were
seduced by the beauty of the station name.

Incidentally, there are two equivalents of this Parisian
cinema platform in London. One is at Charing Cross, where a
platform of the nascent Jubilee Line was opened in 1979 and

closed in 1999, after it had been decided to extend the Jubilee Line in a direction that did not include Charing Cross ('a shocking waste of money', Christian Wolmar observed in *The Subterranean Railway*). Scenes from *Creep*, *Skyfall*, *The Bourne Ultimatum* and *28 Weeks Later* have been shot on that platform. The other is Aldwych, a closed-down station of the Piccadilly opened in 1907 as 'Strand'. A 'theatre shuttle' used to operate from there to Holborn, the Strand being a street of theatres. After its closure in 1994, theatrical productions have been staged at Aldwych, and TV programmes and films were shot there before and after the closure, including *A Run for Your Money* (1949) and *The Clouded Yellow* (1950), which are both good, and *Death Line* (1972), which is not. It's remarkable how often Dr Who's TARDIS materialised at Aldwych, given the inter-galactic range of destinations open to him.

At quarter to twelve on that winter's night in 2001, the platforms were more cinematic than dead. They were filling up with Parisian rail enthusiasts, who looked as dapper and urbane as the standard sort of Parisian, and there were as many women as men, whereas when I went on a tour of the hidden bits of the Victoria Line, all my fellow passengers were men.

I had already suspected that *les passionnés du ferrovaire* were different from their British equivalents. In the Vie du Rail bookshop (slogan: '*Le Monde du Train et du Voyage Intelligent*'), on rue de Clichy near Saint-Lazare station, I had noticed a surprising lightness of tone: almost as many novels, posters and children's books as technical manuals. I once suggested to an assistant in a London transport bookshop, about which I was writing an article, that the books he sold – such as *Tank Engines, Classes L1 to N19* or *Ferries from Pembrokeshire* – were incredibly arcane. He seemed to think those particular titles quite mainstream. 'But the other day,' he continued, 'we had a request for something on the Maryport and Carlisle Railway coal wagons. Now that really *is* obscure.' One of his customers refused to speak to me because the paper I was writing for had used the term 'trainspotter' in a derogatory manner.

In Britain, perhaps as a by-product of the marginalisation of engineering, society has turned against rail enthusiasts, and some rail enthusiasts have turned against society. They send people like me, who presume to broach their pet subjects, letters beginning (without preamble), 'As a railway author myself, I know the importance of factual accuracy ...'

Perhaps I was blinded by my Francophilia, but I couldn't imagine the people milling sociably on the *quai mort* sending letters like that. I got talking to one young man – who turned out (after he'd modestly tried to deflect me from the discovery) to be a concert pianist – whether an interest in trains might be regarded as eccentric in French society. 'Why would that be?' he said. To answer a question with a question is a sign of healthy socialisation, I think. Another man on the platform did the same when I asked him why RATP had dropped the requirement for train drivers to wear a uniform (which occurred in the 1980s, as I had only just discovered). 'Political gesture?' he said, smiling and raising a querulous eyebrow.

We have seen that two tunnels had been built to connect Porte des Lilas to the Line 7 loop, and only one was used. Our first destination lay along the *unused* tunnel (called Voie des Fêtes) on which a station had been constructed below ground, but no ticket hall or surface buildings were ever built. This was – and is – Haxo, a sort of cold Metro cave (the white tiles having been removed years ago) daubed all over with graffiti. From an English-speaker's perspective, Haxo is a good name for such a mysterious location, since it's an anagram of 'hoax'.

After we'd inspected Haxo, to the accompaniment of spookily echoing barrel organ music, played by an ADEMAS man wearing a straw boater, our train returned to Lilas. Here we took advantage of that little-used connection between 3*bis* and 3, whereupon we were free from that cul-de-sac – at liberty to roam over the network, along tunnels with their partial, Halloween illumination, moving through Piranesian galleries (lines going under, lines going over) and through stations where a few bleary '*voyageurs ordinaire*' (as Julian Pepinster pityingly referred to them) still lingered. At 3 a.m., our tour culminated at a depot and driver training centre under Gare du Nord. We were served crisps and glasses of Kir Royale as we filed along underneath our own train, now parked on top of an inspection pit, where ADEMAS boffins were stationed every few yards to answer questions. Soon after that, we were on the Line 2 viaduct looking down at a sleeping Gare du Nord. At 5 a.m., we returned to Porte des Lilas, where croissants and hot chocolate were served.

I have only once eaten decent fare in a British rail-enthusiast setting: a succulent Cornish pasty served during a footplate experience day on the Bodmin & Wenford Railway; otherwise, it's been weak tea and damp biscuits. So I think it worth reporting, by way of illustrating another of those cultural differences, that, just as the Gare du Nord Kir Royale had been correctly chilled, the Lilas croissants were warm and fresh, the hot chocolate rich and creamy.

Line 4

I was always plugged into Paris by Line 4, because it serves Gare du Nord. My impression was of a busy line – it's the second busiest after Line 1 – in the classic Metro style: a snowdrift of consistently white stations, and at the time of writing, it's a showcase for the back-to-basics of Renouveau du Metro.

Line 4 is the main north–south axis of the primary Grand Croisée. It was not fully opened until 1910, because it took Fulgence Bienvenüe longer than he had expected to tunnel under the river. The early Metro lines went over the river, tunnelling technology being primitive at the time, but there could be no question of building railway bridges and viaducts in the very heart of Paris, so Line 4 could never go over the Seine. It also had to be careful what it went *under.* The original planned route would have taken it through the basement of the domed palace on the Quai de Conti belonging to the Institut de France, whose five academies seek to control French intellectual life; but the academicians insisted it be diverted.

In effect the line would have to cross the river twice, because the Seine divides as it flows north and south of the Île de la Cité. Bienvenüe's method – or that of his under-river specialist, Léon Chagnaud – was to encase the stations involved (sited on the riverbanks) and the sub-aqueous part of the line in caissons – steel cages lined with concrete. There is a famous picture (originally a postcard) of what looks like a giant whale skeleton at the north end of boulevard St Michel. The top of it is on a level with the third-storey windows of the adjacent buildings. This is one of the caissons under construction. The under-river ones were towed into the Seine and sunk onto the riverbed. In a chamber of pressurised air at the bottom of the caissons, men dug away until the whole thing descended into the excavation. A great riverside liquid nitrogen factory was built to freeze, and stabilise, the saturated south riverbank for excavation. As the work at the river was continuing, the rest of the line (which is entirely underground) was opened between 1908 and 1910.

Each of the two stations participating in the river crossing, St Michel on the South Bank and Cité on the Île de la Cité, comprise three caissons: two vertical ones at either end for entrances and exits and one lateral one for the platforms. When you're on the platforms, you wouldn't necessarily know you were in a caisson, because the walls have the usual white tiles, but you can sense there's something fishy going on, because the attempt to mimic the traditional, landlocked Metro vault hasn't quite worked. The St Michel and Cité vaults seem distorted, higher than the others, the ellipsis not so relaxed.

The Cité platforms are particularly strange, with lighting

by clusters of white globes, which look as though they might start revolving to demonstrate planetary orbits. You expect some top-hatted, moustachioed man to come along and explain. As for the vertical caissons at the ends, there is no attempt to finesse these: you feel as though you're standing in a great riveted metal bucket, with rusty water dribbling down the sides, and staircases with ornate railings – but still looking as though built in a hurry – ascending in a criss-crossing Escher-like way towards the relative sanity of the ticket hall on the mezzanine level. (You are very aware of the *underneath* of those staircases.)

There are also lifts in the shafts, but these seem like afterthoughts, and most *voyageurs* prefer to walk up, shoes and boots clanging, the Parisians being schooled in staircase climbing. One of the two vertical caissons at Cité is currently out of action, and *voyageurs* are barred from it by railings, but you can still look up it – although you wouldn't want to if you suffered from vertigo. The walls here are roughly plastered, and set high up is a barred window, suggesting a lonely dungeon, and there was, until 1985, a passage connecting this caisson to the Paris Police Headquarters.

At Châtelet station you are clear of the river on the North Bank. The Line 1 part of this sprawling station opened in 1900. Line 7 was diverted to Châtelet in 1934. Line 11 arrived the following year. In 1977 the nearby Châtelet les Halles RER station was opened and connected to Châtelet. Line 14 arrived at Châtelet in 1998, compounding the confusion, which surely persists for most people when emerging from the station, because there are sixteen exits, one of which, at Place Sainte Opportune, boasts a replica Guimard *édicule* dating from 2000.

For more than a century, Line 4 was stable, with Porte de Clignancourt at the top and Porte d'Orléans at the bottom the veritable 'north' and 'south' of the system map. It was always likely that if the line did extend it would go south, its adjacent southern suburbs lobbying more strongly than the less well-off northern ones. But it wasn't until 2013 that Line 4 reached out southwards to Montrouge. (In *The Story of the Paris Metro*, Clive Lamming writes, 'The 40,000 inhabitants of Montrouge felt dislocated from Paris, and a real village atmosphere still prevails today in the small cafés close to the town hall.')

The terminal stations still tyrannise the Paris novice, because of that word 'direction', but on pocket maps from 1988 their names were highlighted: written in white in black boxes, a feature that endured for years. The non-Parisian Metro user becomes intrigued by the names of these end-points to which he or she is perpetually directed but will probably never visit, since they are remote from the tourist spots, whether they be inside or just outside Paris proper. As the network has groped its way into the suburbs the names of the termini have changed, which is disorientating to the occasional visitor.

For forty years after I first used the Metro, the co-ordinates for me – given that I would always start from Gare du Nord Line 4 – were Porte de Clignancourt and Porte d'Orléans. I shunned Clignancourt because that would take me north.

Orléans was the one for me, since that lay south, the direction of Odéon station in the 6th Arrondissement where, by force of habit, I alighted and made for one of the many three-star hotels nearby. (Three-star is about my speed.) Odéon was fixed in my mind because the station exit lies at a junction in front of a cinema, which, being British, I thought of as an Odeon, whereas in fact the station name denotes something grander: the nearby Odéon Theatre, which dates from 1819. (That said, many Metro stations are at junctions, where Parisian cinemas also tend to occur, in sociable early-evening conjunction.)

In 2013, I lost my Porte d'Orléans reference point, when Line 4 made its leap to Mairie de Montrouge. I felt bereaved, despite never having been to Porte d'Orléans, and I thought I had better see the opposite pole, Porte de Clignancourt, before that too was superseded by an extension. In 2016 or so, I stayed on the train beyond Odéon and went right to the end. Having always enjoyed saying 'Clignancourt' because of the sinuous fluidity of all those French vowels, I expected a place that would be somehow attractive.

On a hot, grey day I emerged amid traffic roar next to my least favourite type of Metro totem: not one of Guimard's flowery extravaganzas, but one of the yellow capital Ms in a circle, which originated in the 1950s, became widespread in the Seventies, and which look plastic-y to me – too reminiscent of the McDonalds logo. Atop the M sat an ill-looking pigeon. It was adjacent to a typical Parisian café terrace, albeit with a clientele of depressed-looking smokers, but on the north side of the road that skirted the café terrace, boulevard Ney, a shocking thing had occurred: Paris had come to an end; reality had taken over.

I was looking at a sort of low-rise shanty town of burger joints and cheap clothes shops. They had to be low-rise because some of them squatted beneath a bridge carrying an uglier thoroughfare even than boulevard Ney, and one still less deserving of the noble designation 'Boulevard', namely the Boulevard Périphérique, that dystopian motorway encircling Paris and forming an unconscious perpetuation of the Thiers Wall, whose course it follows. (In the *Financial Times Magazine* on 14 March 2022, Simon Kuper wrote that the Périphérique divides Paris from its suburbs 'like a moat'.) I crossed the boulevard Ney, which was not easy, and watched as cars swerved off it onto a slip-road of the Périphérique, which they accelerated towards as though joining a race. At the end of the slip road I could see the multi-lanes of the Périphérique, like a giant, real-life computer game.

The first section of the Périphérique opened in 1960; it completed its circuit of Paris in 1973. On 22 November 1972, *Paris Soir* had described it as 'an inferno', a 'ring of death'. It's not something you'd want to be exposed to for long, but I suppose most people could stand it for 11 minutes and 4 seconds. That's how long a mysterious French stunt motorcyclist known as Pascal the Black Prince took to complete the full circuit of 35 kilometres with a camera strapped to his petrol tank one night in 1989. The film is on YouTube, and the hellish nature of the road, with its oppressive low overpasses and glaring yellow lights, is compounded by the migraine screech of the bike and the bleak viewers' comments below: 'This was at night, does not count'; 'As far as I know, he died while trying to beat his Périphérique record. Crashed into a truck'; 'Other sources say he died in Brussels.'

Students of fast illegal driving might compare the more famous short film, *C'était un Rendez-Vous*, made in 1976 by the French film director Claude Lelouch. This is more attractive because it begins as he *leaves* the wretched Périphérique, via a tunnel at Porte Dauphine beside the Bois de Boulogne in west Paris. He races with much squealing of brakes (a sound effect added later, apparently, which is not to say he's not going fast) past most of the famous bits of Paris at dawn: up Avenue Foch to the Arc de Triomphe … Champs-Élysées … Place Concorde … past the Tuileries and the Louvre into the middle of town … In the violet-tinged light of a Parisian dawn, the red traffic lights (and the occasional green one) glow prettily as he passes. The trip ends in Montmartre at the steps of the Sacré-Coeur, where a beautiful blonde flutters up to greet our leather-jacketed hero, hence the title – and we viewers of a certain age do expect to see the caption, 'And all because the lady loves Milk Tray …'

Just in case any true petrolhead should have strayed into reading a book on the Metro, I should add that the vehicle in the film is reputed to be a Mercedes 450SEL 6.9, with sound dubbed from a V12 Ferrari. To be fair to Lelouch, he said he would have slowed down or even stopped had any pedestrian got in his way.

*

In 2022, Line 4 was extended south again by a further two stations: Barbara and Bagneux-Lucie Aubrac, the latter poised for connection to Line 15 of the Grand Paris Express. As a terminal name, Bagneux-Lucie Aubrac is not as resonant as Porte d'Orléans, whereas 'Barbara' simply feels foreshortened. It commemorates a French singer, Monique Andrée Serf (1930–97), who, like Morrissey or Adele, was known by only one name. Being Jewish, Barbara had to go into hiding during the war, and this traumatised her for life. As her Wikipedia page has it: 'A tall person, Barbara dressed in black as she sang melancholy songs of lost love.' She is buried in the cemetery at Bagneux, near the station named in her honour. She was one of those unexportable French stars, like Serge Gainsbourg or Johnny Hallyday, and why a Metro station hasn't been named after *him* I can't think. Perhaps because he made his home in LA?

Line 4, which is fully automated (no drivers), is the second busiest after Line 1, partly because it serves Gare de l'Est and Gare du Nord, and there always seems to be a collective exhalation after Gare du Nord on the northbound trains. Line 4 connects to all other Metro lines except those anti-social twins 7*bis* and 3*bis*.

Lines 5 and 6

The theatrical highlight of Line 5 – and perhaps the entire Metro – is its river crossing, between Gare de l'Austerlitz on the South Bank and Quai de la Rapée on the North. The performance begins three stations south of Austerlitz, at the southern terminus, Place d'Italie, where the line begins (or ends) on one of those passenger-carrying loops that give you the thrill of being admitted backstage. The line comes above ground after Saint-Marcel, with the Jardin des Plantes arrayed to your left. The train then outrageously enters, through a sky-light, the roof of Gare d'Austerlitz, where the Line 5 station of that name is located, and it's as though you have come across the full-sized trainset kept in an attic, what with all the steel beams resembling rafters. The train leaves the Austerlitz roof through another skylight, in order to cross the river on the elegant, single-span Viaduc d'Austerlitz, created by those two Metro-dramatists, Louis Biette and Jean-Camille Formigé, who also created the Line 2 and 6 viaducts, and Pont de Bir-Hakeim at the western end of the latter.

As the trains descend towards the next station, Quai de la Rapée on the North Bank, they swirl with misplaced exuberance around the Paris morgue, otherwise known as the Institut Médico-Légal, a brick building that does its best to look anonymous on the riverbank. (Its address, by the way, is 2 Voie Mazas, not 'Rue Morgue'. There never was a rue Morgue in Paris, despite the imagination of Edgar Allan Poe.) This downhill stretch is known as 'the toboggan', and after you've ridden it once, perhaps while looking left, where Notre-Dame seems to be marching towards you, you immediately want to do it again in the opposite direction, and if you look left *this* time, the austere skyscrapers of the Bibliothèque François Mitterrand command the scene, because Paris is modern in that direction.

In performing this leap, Line 5 only just misses Gare de Lyon, which lies a few hundred metres to the east, and the question is *why* does Line 5 miss Gare de Lyon, which for many years was poorly served by the Metro? (Only Line 1 went there.) The answer is that Line 5 was originally intended to share the tunnels of Line 1 in order to curve right to Gare de Lyon, but the plan was abandoned as being impure and inelegant – a shame, in a way, because Austerlitz and Lyon do form a partnership of sorts. Anyone looking confused while seeking to board a main-line train at Gare d'Austerlitz is asked by station staff whether they really ought to be in the station over the river – Gare de Lyon, from where, as from Austerlitz, trains head south.

If you stay on Line 5 after Quai de la Rapée, you will arrive at Bastille on a platform incorporating part of the foundations of the prison stormed in the Revolution, that were discovered when Line 5 reached Bastille in 1905, and I suppose some long-serving commuters might consider the station was a perpetuation of the gaol.

The early history of Line 5, which opened in 1906, is so fraught that I refuse point blank to describe it. Let's just say that, until 1942, it incorporated the southern curvature – that 'southern smile' – that today belongs to Line 6. It also stretched a long way north, so that it was an upside-down scythe shape.

In 1985, after forty years of stasis, Line 5 was extended further north, by a long, overground section, to Bobigny-Pantin-Raymond Queneau, named after the nearby rue

Raymond Queneau, which is in turn named after the author of *Zazie Dans Le Metro*. Apparently, the station will soon be served by something called the T Zen Network, a new bus rapid transit system. Queneau would have been pleased, since he was an odd combination of Modernist experimentalist and public transport nerd. His most famous novel apart from *Zazie* is *Exercises in Style*, which describes an altercation on a Paris bus ninety-nine different ways.

After the station named in Queneau's honour (I can't be bothered to repeat the title) comes the terminus Bobigny-Pablo Picasso, which awaits Line 15 of the Grand Paris Express. Why all this Bobigny action? At the time of the Line 5 extension, it had recently gone up in the world, having become the *préfecture*, or administrative headquarters, of Seine-Saint Denis, poorest of the three *départements* immediately outside Paris, known as the Petit-Couronne.

The above-mentioned stations are lined with small white tiles embellished with very wide coloured strips, in red and orange respectively. On the way to the terminus you pass on your left the Bobigny depot, where Line 5 trains (the swish MF 01s) are stabled. This gives a rare opportunity to see Metro trains assembled en masse in the open air, because usually they're tucked away out of sight in sidings and loops at the ends of the lines. Accordingly, the trains look out of their element in a faintly disturbing way: like seeing fish on a slab rather than swimming in the sea.

*

As for Line 6, we have already discussed it in relation to Line 2, its approximate mirror image on the North Bank, and we have seen how it grew out of Line 5.

At the western end, it emerges from a tunnel at Passy on the North Bank for a run of six elevated stations, beginning with the river crossing on Pont de Bir-Hakeim. This, the masterpiece of Biette and Formigé, commands superb views of the adjacent Eiffel Tower – and of course Parisian *voyageurs* don't look up from their smartphones. ('Zone', a poem of 1917 by Guillaume Apollinaire, implies that the Eiffel Tower is shepherdess to the Parisian bridges.)

Bir-Hakeim – 'I would trade in the Champs-Élysées for it any day', wrote Ian Nairn – is a bridge on a bridge. The lower deck is a road and walkway; the upper deck, which carries the Metro, rests on great stanchions like an avenue of iron trees, which becomes something more akin to an enchanted forest when the antique-looking lanterns hanging from it are lit – and these lanterns continue along the ornate viaducts that follow. You could say there were in fact three dimensions to the bridge, if you include the boats gliding past below, or walkers on the *quais*. The film *Fear over the City* adds yet another dimension in that Jean-Paul Belmondo, as a cop pursuing a villain, walks along the top of a Line 6 train as it crosses the bridge; he then has to quickly lie flat, losing some of his dignity in the process, as the train approaches Bir-Hakeim station, because while that is elevated, it's not open to the air: it has a glass roof.

To turn to more serious cinema, I have said that *Last Tango in Paris* is a great Metro film. It is, in particular, a great Line 6 film. It begins with Marlon Brando on the Pont de Bir-Hakeim walkway, screaming with whatever existential angst he is suffering from (the film never made this clear to me) as a Metro train rumbles overhead. The implication is that it's the train that brings on his anxiety – so why does he then rent a flat (the one he will share with Maria Schneider) on rue Jules Verne, which directly overlooks the part of the Line 6 viaduct we are discussing? Probably because Bertolucci kept wanting to show the trains – symbols, perhaps, of the transience and anonymity that characterise the film's central relationship.

I once discussed this part of town with a woman in her sixties whose mother lived in a third-floor flat on boulevard de Grenelle, directly overlooking the Line 6 viaduct. She insisted that such flats are no cheaper than any others in the desirable 15th Arrondissement, and that her mother enjoyed being near the trains, but did admit that her mother might have been prejudiced, since her (the mother's) father had been one of the first drivers on the Metro. The boulevards and Line 6 do seem to have reached an accommodation, like two grand, venerable families; once, perhaps, wary of one another, but with more and more in common as time goes by.

After that first elevated stretch, Line 6 proceeds as follows: underground, overground, underground, overground including the second crossing of the Seine, on Pont de Bercy (which seems another bridge-on-a-bridge, albeit entirely of stone, but is in fact three bridges side-by-side, opened in 1864, 1909 and 1991), then underground again for the final run to Nation, which we have already visited.

Line 6 trains are those rubber-shod seniors the MP73s, which have rather worn-out interiors in a colour scheme of sickly 1970s green, which I quite like. On the viaducts, however, I'm looking through the windows, and my mind is on Paris, not the train.

Line 7

Line 7, which opened in 1910, is a most un-Metro-like affair. Its north–south course is long; some of its stations lie deep, and it has a working-class clientele, by virtue of northern extensions of the late 1970s out to Fort d'Aubervilliers, where it will be connected to Line 15 of the Grand Paris Express.

By this, Line 7 was reaching out to some of the most deprived areas the Metro had yet encountered, where inter-war HBM blocks (*habitations à bon marché*) had lately given way to their 1960s and 1970s equivalents, *habitations à loyer modéré* (HLM). I am speaking here of the main northern branch of the line, but there is another, and Line 7 is additionally untypical because it has branches at its northern and southern ends.

The north-end bifurcation occurred in 1911, when an eastern prong sprouted and culminated in a multi-station loop. I mentioned this loop when discussing Line 3, which was tenuously connected to it by a shuttle service.

In 1967, the lack of *voyageurs* on the loop meant it suffered the same demeaning fate that would befall the Gambetta-Lilas stretch of Line 3. It became self-contained as 7*bis*, condemned to using old stock, while the main northern branch to Porte de la Villette got new trains and a busier timetable. We will be visiting the loop shortly, but first let us consider depth.

The deepest station is Buttes Chaumont, on 7*bis* up towards the loop: its platforms are 29 metres below the surface. (The deepest station on the entire Metro is Abbesses, which lies beneath the Montmartre hill, 36 metres down.)

There are more than 200 steps at Buttes Chaumont, which would trigger a warning 'use-staircase-only-in-emergency' sign on the London Underground, even though that system is much deeper (Hampstead, for example, is about twice as deep as Buttes Chaumont). This being Paris, there is a drama to the depth, and there are seats on the landings between the flights of stairs at Buttes Chaumont, inviting *voyageurs* to take a rest. There is also a lift, I should add, and perhaps it is widely favoured over the stairs. Anyhow, I have never seen anyone else on them.

We are in the lonely, hilly north-east again, where abandoned gypsum and limestone quarries – so many white, honeycombed grottoes – created unnatural ridges in the landscape and tested the ingenuity even of Bienvenüe and his men. There is a thick central wall between the two platforms at Buttes Chaumont, to strengthen the vault, but as usual when this is done, the builders have atoned for departing from the classic arrangement by providing a hole in the wall so you can see at least a bit of the opposite platform, and with luck there might be people on it.

You might need that reassurance at Buttes Chaumont, which is a creepy station, one of the four quietest on the network.

The station serves Buttes Chaumont Park, opened in 1867 on a territory blighted by quarrying below and perhaps also spiritually: it accommodated firstly a gallows, then a great rubbish dump, then various noxious and smelly trades like tannery, glue- and soap-making. Buttes-Chaumont was 'engineered', being a very man-made park, by Adolphe Alphand, head of the Parks Department under Haussmann. It is thought that Fulgence Bienvenüe contributed to some structural work at the park after it opened.

It's a warped arcadia, the main feature being a mock Roman temple propped on top of an artificial cliff, like a wedding cake decoration. There's a grotto beneath, blasted out of the remains of a gypsum quarry; an artificial waterfall crashes down through it to an equally artificial lake. It seems somehow logical that the Charlie Hebdo killers convened to plot hereabouts.

If you happen to be a rail enthusiast, the park is notable for accommodating a mildewed cutting through which the Petite Ceinture once ran. This circular railway was conceived by Napoleon III, who definitely *was* a rail enthusiast, for military-strategic reasons: to connect the outlying railway termini (and in particular their goods stations), so the Ceinture was a state rather than a city project. But the Metro – a city project conceived in *opposition* to the state – would have its revenge. In 1900, the first year of the Metro, the Ceinture carried 339 million passengers. But, owing to the success of the Metro, by 1927 that figure was down to seven million, and over the next decades the Ceinture slowly died. Among the last passenger trains using it were those operated by the Wagons-Lits company, transferring wealthy Britons from Gare du Nord to the Gare de Lyon, en route to the Riviera.

About five years ago, I was looking wistfully down at this cutting (in which the railway tracks remain) as a photographer – or at least a man with a fancy camera – scrambled down the bank into it. I attempted to inquire, in French, whether he was trespassing. He answered in English (as the French tend to do when I speak to them in their language): 'This is France; a lot of things are illegal.' Not wanting to appear a wimp, I followed him down, but didn't penetrate very far into the shadowy tunnel at the southern end of the cutting that leads under the streets of the 20th Arrondissement. The photographer did, his voice echoing back to me a modification of his earlier pronouncement: 'This is France ... You do what you want.'

'Trains run in both directions every ten minutes,' says *Baedeker's Paris*, 1904 edition, of the Ceinture,

and take 1 hr. 40 min. to perform the circuit. The chief station of arrival and departure is the Gare Saint-Lazare. Travellers may avail themselves of this railway as an alternative to the Metropolitain, to visit points of interest in the suburbs, such as the Bois de Boulogne, Pere Lachaise and the Buttes-Chaumont, or to make the complete circuit of the city. On every side of the town, however, except the S.W., the line runs between walls or through deep cuttings and tunnels. The seats on the outside (*'impériale'*) are scarcely to be recommended; they are very draughty and exposed to dust and smoke.

In Parc Montsouris, in south Paris, there is another ghostly cutting that once accommodated the line.

Progressing one stop further east from Buttes Chaumont, we come to the big, visible-on-the-map 7*bis* loop, and the classic two-platform vault is absent from all four stations on it because, being deep, they needed reinforcement. There is further strangeness at Danube and Place des Fêtes. The former rests on great, 30-metre-tall stone stilts, because there's an old quarry – that is, a void – beneath it. The one time I got off at Danube, I thought I detected a hollow resonance to the arriving and departing trains – even to the footsteps of the few *voyageurs* – but it was probably just my imagination. Place des Fêtes has a small but striking Art Deco surface building resembling an Art Deco flat iron and dating from 1935, when Line 11 arrived at the station. (You can see this entrance – with police cars pulling up outside – in the Metro chase sequence of the film *Le Samouraï*.) In that politically unstable decade, it was added as part of work to make the station sealable against a gas attack. The overall effect of the 7*bis* stations is of being in small spaces amid oppressive, thick whiteness, as if one were snowbound, or in the heart of a glacier.

In 1982, by the way, the southern branch of Line 7 was opened. This reached its present southern terminus, Villejuif

Louis Aragon, in 1985, and here it awaits the Line 15 of the
Grand Paris Express.

Lines 8, 9 and 10

Line 8 is not very famous, but its advocates might argue that
it has three *claims* to fame. The first is modest: it's tangled up
with Line 9 as it runs through the heart of the North Bank,
serving the *Grands Boulevards*, that district of theatres (from
the Opéra to the Folies Bergère), theatrical restaurants, cinemas and glitzy shops, most of whose sybaritic patrons (whether
tourists or Parisians) do not consider the weird arrangements
of the Metro lines that convey them to their pleasures.

The second claim is not much to Line 8's credit: it was the
scene of the first Metro murder. The third claim is the sheer
prolongation of the line's extension to the south-eastern suburbs, which Clive Lamming describes as 'seemingly endless'.

We will discuss the eccentricity of the entangled central
stretch when we come to Line 9. But let's say for now that it
arises from CMP plans of 1907 for an 'additional network' of
the Metro, which included the idea of an inner circle, straddling
the North and South Banks, from Invalides to Invalides, via
Saint-Germain, Bastille, République and Opéra. The plan was
never carried through in that form; it went against Bienvenüe's
notion of elegance, or, as Brian Hardy writes in *Paris Metro
Handbook*, 'perhaps someone came to London and had a close
look at the complex workings of the Inner Circle!' But the ghost

of the circular idea survived and would influence the creation of Lines 8, 9 and 10. Even Brian Hardy, a master of Metro detail, seems to quail slightly at the prospect of describing 8, 9 and 10 ('The history of these three lines is rather complex').

Line 8 opened in 1913, running none too purposefully from Opéra on the North Bank towards the south-west of the South Bank. To cut a long and involved story short, it had reached the suburb of Balard down there in the south-west by 1937, and that remains one of its termini.

The other end of the line – having been extended east of Opéra in the late 1920s – also began to aim south, so Line 8 was developing the look of a droopy moustache. By 1931, it had curved down to Porte de Charenton on the south-east corner of the North Bank, and this was another case of Expo motivation for the Metro, because Porte de Charenton would serve the Paris Colonial Exposition of 1931, which was staged in the nearby Bois de Vincennes. That Expo featured a scenic railway roller-coaster that was acquired the following year by Great Yarmouth Pleasure Beach, where it is still in use, albeit shorn of its original scenery, which had suggested an alpine setting: wooden mountains, a model castle. (You don't need artificial scenery at Great Yarmouth, because you've got the North Sea.) It's a rattly wooden ride controlled by an actual person – a brakeman – so you get a ride that he or she considers exciting-but-safe; that their benchmark might differ from yours of course adds to the excitement. (You can see this coaster in the video to Madness's song, 'House of Fun'.)

Porte de Charenton was still the terminus of Line 8 on 16

May 1937, when (surprisingly belatedly) the first Metro murder
happened thereabouts ...

The victim was Laetitia Toureaux, and it's surprising that her
story hasn't been turned into a feature film, not least because she
looked like a film star. Toureaux was a young Italian immigrant,
bright, dynamic and with multiple identities, which could be
useful – or dangerous – in the febrile political atmosphere of late
1930s France under the Popular Front government, which was
not popular with the right. Her day job was in a wax factory.
She also worked as a cloakroom attendant and dance partner
for hire at a louche *bal musette*, or dance hall. She also appears
to have been a *mouchard*, or spy, for hire, and was on the books
of a private detective agency. It's thought she spied on her fellow
workers at the wax factory and reported any insubordination
to the bosses, and she kept tabs on her fellow immigrants, on
behalf of the Italian Embassy. It also seems likely she had infil-
trated, on behalf of the police, a right-wing antisemitic terrorist
organisation, the Comité Secret d'Action Revolutionnaire, aka
La Cagoule, a reference to their cowled headgear. The Cagoule
had connections in French industrial and political high society.
In 1937, Marx Dormoy, Minister of the Interior, mounted a raid
that fatally undermined the organisation. Dormoy would be
assassinated – most likely by Cagoulards – in 1941 while under
house arrest by the Vichy government, some of whose members
were ex-Cagoulards. (The name of Marx Dormoy adorns a Line
12 Metro station that we will be visiting.)

What happened to Laetitia Toureaux was this.

On the evening of 16 May 1937, she took a bus from the dance hall where she worked to Porte de Charenton Metro station. It was a hot, rainy night. In their gripping book about the case, *Murder in the Metro*, Gayle K. Brunelle and Annette Finley-Croswhite evoke the atmosphere nicely, although they do seem to have forgotten that Metro trains were electric even then:

> Toureaux was not alone at the Porte de Charenton. It was Pentecost, a Catholic holy day and a long holiday weekend for even the most overburdened of the Parisian working class. The unexpected thunderstorm had driven many of the picknickers and strollers who had been enjoying the unusually warm afternoon in the Parc de Vincennes to take cover in the Metro. The damp underground air reeked of stale perspiration and the nauseating odour of soot from the trains.

As she waited for a train to take her in the direction of town (the only direction, given that Porte de Charenton was a terminus), Laetitia Toureaux stood on the part of the platform that would align with the first-class car. 'The first-class car, it is important to note, was not widely used,' explain Brunelle and Finley-Croswhite, 'because it cost more than most people could afford in Depression-era France. While it was reserved for wealthier travellers, it was also used by high-class prostitutes in search of well-paying clients.' Their point is not that Laetitia Toureaux was a prostitute (she was not), but that people were curious about who went into the first-class cars, and they paid attention. Witnesses would attest that Toureaux alone was waiting for the first-class car, and that she alone had entered it when the train departed at 6.27 p.m. At 6.28 p.m. (a typical Metro interval), the train arrived at the next stop, Porte Dorée, where Laetitia Toureaux was discovered by a family entering the first-class car dying with a 9-inch knife in her neck.

The case was a sensation at the time, and apparently remains a taboo subject in France, as embarrassingly revealing of rightist politics in high society. There's a photograph online of a smartly dressed man (presumably a detective) crouching over the pool of blood on the carriage floor and grinning at the sheer drama of it. Possibly because of political sensitivities, the case was dropped in 1939; nobody was ever convicted of the killing. The likeliest culprit was Jean Filiol, an unshaven, brutish-looking man in a shapeless hat (going by an online photograph), who died in exile in Spain some time after the war – and even if he didn't do the crime, it's his own fault he's in the frame, because his job title (more or less) was assassin for La Cagoule.

I have an interest in crime fiction, of which one sub-genre is the 'locked-room mystery' – apparently impossible crimes, begging the question: how did the murderer get in or out? The first example of these has a Parisian setting: 'The Murders in the Rue Morgue', by Edgar Allan Poe. (Spoiler alert: an orangutan did it.) On one website devoted to locked-room mysteries, the murder of Laetitia Toureaux is cited among real-life examples.

*

In 1942, Line 8 pushed beyond Porte de Charenton to Charenton-Écoles. Nothing happened to it for a while after that, and very little to the Metro generally. But Line 8 would pioneer the 1970s Metro extensions as it reached towards, and crossed, the Marne River, to serve Créteil, one of the new towns created on the outskirts of Paris in the 1960s. The stations on the extension have pale yellow or beige flat tiles redolent of the 1970s, and the bleak MF77 trains of Line 8 seem very at home in these.

When I rode this end of Line 8 in mid-2022, it occurred to me that I had been to École Vétérinaire des Maisons-Alfort station about twenty years earlier to write an article, and here we are in for another macabre Line 8 reflection. The piece was about the Fragonard Museum, sited in an annex of the veterinary school and named after its first professor of anatomy, Honoré Fragonard. Here, flayed preserved cadavers are displayed, including human foetuses in dancing poses or riding the foetuses of cows or sheep, and – most notoriously – an exhibit called 'The Horseman of the Apocalypse': the staring corpse of a man on an equally dead horse. Fragonard, deemed mad for the theatricality of his anatomical experiments, was dismissed from the college. It's interesting to speculate that there might be some modern-day student, a disciple of his, riding daily to the veterinary school on Line 8 and imagining what his or her fellow *voyageurs* would look like without their skin.

At Créteil-L'Échat, Line 8 will be connected to Line 15 of the Grand Paris Express. There follows a run along the central reservation of a motorway, the A4 – Metro-dramatic, yes, but by the time I had reached the anonymous above-ground terminus at Créteil Pointe du Lac (added to the line in 2011), I had almost forgotten I was on the Metro. The train driver seemed a bit bemused as well because when, as he emerged from his cab, I sought to double-check that we had just crossed the Marne and not the Seine, he frowned and said, 'I *think* we crossed the Seine ...' We had not, though; we'd crossed the Marne.

Between 1970 and 1982, a supplementary fare was charged for travelling over this long stretch, so that was a twelve-year departure from Metro elegance, and there was nearly another one, when it was proposed that some trains along the stretch should be 'express' – that is, skipping certain stops. But this never came to pass, and such stressful innovations would be left to the RER.

Whereas Line 8 straddles the North and South Banks in a conceptually messy way, Line 9 is all on the North Bank, and more associated with the high life of the *Grands Boulevards* than Line 8, even though both serve that glamorous territory.

Let's take Bonne Nouvelle station, whose name, as shown on the platforms, has been designed by the Metro's 'Department of Humour' in such a way that all the letters are at different levels, in the manner of the Hollywood sign, to acknowledge the proximity of the massive Grand Rex Cinema (model for the Radio City Music Hall in New York), whose history is a history of cinema itself ... If you asked most Parisians to name the line on which this station stands, they'd probably say Line 9, even though it is served by both 8 and 9. But the former is reputationally weighted down, as it were, by its long, dreary (or hypnotic) south-eastern extension.

Line 9 was opened in 1922. By the next year, it stretched east from Porte de Saint-Cloud to Chaussée d'Antin in the heart of the North Bank. I have mentioned that Line 8 had been extended east of Opéra in the late 1920s. In fact, in the late 1920s and early 1930s, Lines 8 and 9 were extended *together* in that direction from Chaussée d'Antin to République, encompassing Richelieu-Drouot, Grands Boulevards, Bonne Nouvelle, Strasbourg Saint-Denis and Saint-Martin stations on the way, all of which are served by both lines – and it was indeed part of the 1907 'additional network' plan that these two lines would run together over the top of the notional inner circle.

It's a strange arrangement, though, or you might say typically imaginative. The classic station vault is largely banished on this stretch, with westbound and eastbound platforms separated by walls, and the Line 9 platforms below and *between* the Line 8 ones. I would recommend that readers go and see for themselves, but even then all may not be clear. Things are so arranged to minimise the lateral space taken up by the two lines. The separating walls also reinforce the stations, which are built in marshy ground. The stacked arrangement means that there are many exits from these stations – many opportunities for *voyageurs* to flee these subterranean complications in pursuit of surface frivolities.

Between Strasbourg Saint-Denis and République on this

stretch lies an abandoned station, Saint-Martin, one of the many (more than half the network) closed in 1939 as part of wartime Metro retrenchment. Most of those closures were soon reversed, but a dozen stations remained shut immediately after the war. Gradually, these began to be re-opened after lobbying from local residents, but four wallflower stations found too few advocates, and Saint-Martin was one. The trouble was that Strasbourg Saint-Denis station was only 100 metres away, too close even for a Metro station.

I visited Saint-Martin on the nocturnal ADEMAS trip. I recall some faded posters surviving amid the graffiti, one advertising a furrier, another a disinfectant, personified by a green homunculus. One of the Line 8 platforms at Saint-Martin is walled off from the tracks, and the best view of the station is on Line 9, direction Pont de Sèvres (or 'westbound' if you're British). It looms large and graffiti-covered – a shocking, if fleeting, glimpse of dereliction in this smart part of town. In 2010, the station was used to display – and advertise – Nissan Qashqai cars. According to Wikipedia, 'Bees have been flying around this station since the 1980s.'

I have said that Line 9 is associated with all the excitements of downtown Paris, but it, like Line 8, does have its long tail. Whereas Line 8 pioneered the 1970s extensions, as we have just been seeing, Line 9 had pioneered the extensions of the 1930s, in 1934 becoming the first line to cross the city boundary, when it was extended south-west from Porte de Saint-Cloud to Pont de Sèvres. It was aiming here at the Renault factory, newly built on Seguin Island of the Seine, a world away from the *Grands Boulevards*, and the early morning trains in that direction would have been crowded with workmen clutching their baguette-with-slab-of-cheese and bottle of rough red. Porte de Saint-Cloud remains the line's western terminus, but the stopped clock will be re-started when Pont de Sèvres is connected to Line 15 of the Grand Paris Express.

In 1937 Line 9 was also extended east beyond the city boundary from République to Mairie de Montreuil, which remains its eastern terminus.

The first part of today's Line 10 was envisaged as forming the southern part of the proposed inner circle, but by the time the number 10 first appeared on the Metro map, in 1923, it had been decided to confine the line to the South Bank. What follows is a fairly comprehensive (therefore skippable) enumerated history of the line's development, provided to show the incessant fiddling that went on during the evolution of the Metro's 'additional network'.

In 1923, the line ran south from Invalides to Duroc over what is now a part of Line 13.

It then immediately (and bizarrely) headed north-eastwards (forming a 'V' shape), using what is still part of Line 10, to a station called Croix Rouge, one of the 'wallflowers', which closed in 1939 and never re-opened. (Croix Rouge lies between the present Line 10 stations of Sèvres Babylone and Mabillon, and can be seen from passing trains, the station name still defiantly proclaimed in white on blue amid all the graffiti.)

By 1930, Line 10 had drifted further east, along a stretch
that is also still part of the line, to Maubert Mutualité.

In the next year, it was extended from there directly south
to Porte de Choisy on the edge of town.

But this stretch was only part of Line 10 for a matter of
months before it was transferred to Line 7.

What Line 10 lost to the south, however, it would gain to the
west in 1937, when a new stretch was built from the bottom of
the Line 10 'V' at Duroc.

When Line 10 reached La Motte Picquet Grenelle on this
stretch, it connected with, and took over, the western end of
what had been Line 8, which featured a big multi-station loop.
(Not wanting to over-burden the reader with the kind of ped-
antry currently underway, I glossed over the emergence of this
loop when describing Line 8, but we will be visiting it shortly,
and it is highly Metro-dramatic.)

I do hope all this is perfectly clear, by the way? Only a little
way to go.

To the east, Line 10 was extended beyond Maubert Mutualité
to Cardinal Lemoine, then Jussieu, then under the Jardin des
Plantes to Gare d'Austerlitz, which it reached in 1939, and
which remains its easterly terminus. The stretch from Jussieu
to Austerlitz is almost a kilometre long – the longest distance
between two Metro stops until the extensions of 1970s.

There was, thank God, only one subsequent addition to
Line 10, which came in 1980, when it was extended beyond the
above-mentioned big loop to Boulogne Pont de Saint-Cloud,

where it terminates in a great orange box – that colour, long fetishised on the Metro, being still just about in vogue at the time.

My habitual base, in the vicinity of Odéon, is served by Line 10 (as well as Line 4). I would sometimes ride it five stops east, to Gare d'Austerlitz, perhaps to take a sleeper train to Nice: the service known until 2003, when the French depressingly abandoned the naming of trains, as the Train Bleu. As though permanently convalescing after the stresses of its creation, Line 10 is a quiet line, less used than all but the two '*bis*' runts. There's something ghostly about it, since some of the tunnels are painted white, and the paint is flaking off, as in an old house. It always seems to be Sunday on Line 10, except on those Saturdays when the raucous Paris Saint-Germain football fans use it to access the Parc des Princes at the western end, and Austerlitz has in recent years been a sleepy station, not served by any TGVs: a fitting terminus for such faded phenomena as slow night trains. At the time of writing, Line 10 uses the second oldest stock on the Metro, the MF67s.

But let's now go in the opposite direction: towards the famous loop.

At Mirabeau – the strangest station, perhaps, on *any* metro – Line 10 splits for the loop to begin.

At Mirabeau, you can only *board* trains that are coming off the loop and heading back towards town, but you can also *see* the trains coming *from* town and heading onto the loop, and as they do this, they climb, because they have just come from underneath the river. What you see from the single platform is the track immediately in front of you (where a train will eventually arrive to take you off the loop), beyond which is a track on a steep ramp. This ramp is tiled in white, although with embellishments in the form of two horizontal lines, red and green, which gradually diverge, as if to further undermine the notion of horizontality. The trains heading for the loop go roaring up that ramp while paying no attention at all to the station, as if they existed in a parallel universe, their minds on literally higher things, and, since they are tilted, you can see all the sparks fizzing about their undersides like fireflies.

The discrepancy between the horizontal platform on which you stand and the angled bank opposite is alarming, like the kind of chaos left behind by an earthquake, and the scene is made even stranger because Mirabeau, like most stations on the Line 10 loop, is quiet, with − between trains − the air of a morgue about its low-lit, clammy looking white tiles and utilitarian steel light fittings. I don't know which is more compelling: to watch trains on the Mirabeau climb from the platform, or to be aboard one of them, because, as they tilt, there's a sense they're going to crash into the station roof. You can buy postcards showing trains on the Mirabeau ramp, and they cater to a morbid interest, just as the postcards showing Bienvenüe's excavations once did. Mirabeau, to repeat, is not actually on the loop (even though on Metro maps it looks as if it is); it precedes it. There are five stations on the loop, and here, as on the 7*bis* loop, trains run anti-clockwise, and the classic station vault with opposing platforms has been abandoned in favour of more complicated arrangements.

The whole of the loop, which serves the stately streets of the 16th Arrondissement, has an exclusive, incestuous air, owing to the quietness of the stations, and the similarity of their names, which include Église d'Auteuil, Michel-Ange Auteuil, Michel-Ange Molitor. (Line 10 is described by Stephen Clarke in *Paris Revealed* as 'a posh people's line that goes through the Latin Quarter and out into the wilds of the 16th Arrondissement, where it is used only by nannies, old ladies and rich schoolkids who haven't yet been given a Vespa'.)

Wherever Francophile rail enthusiasts are gathered, they will speak of the Line 10 loop. It features in B. J. Prigmore's book *On Rails Under Paris* as among the places to visit on a day out on the Metro, in a chapter called 'Your short holiday in Paris'. The suggestions for the 'day out' are preceded by some general tips for the railway-oriented visitor to Paris, and here Mr Prigmore shows himself to be a man of austere tastes. His 'specifically recommended' cafés include 'Wimpy self-service, half right opposite the main exit from Gare du Nord (useful for 11.30 lunch on the day of return) ... Water is on the tables; other drinks are an extravagance.' The 'day out' itself is not actually written by Mr Prigmore, but by his French friend, P. Malterre. ('His essay has been edited but lightly, to preserve the wit and charm of his near-perfect English.')

Monsieur Malterre devotes several paragraphs to the Line

10 loop. He writes that 'When arriving in the Angel-Molitor [*sic*] station, if you see a row of cars on the right track, you had better alight and look at them. Usually, cars parked here are on the scrap list and you will never see them again.' (The book is full of lamentations for the fading away of the Sprague stock trains.) M. Malterre focusses particularly on Mirabeau, 'a most worthwhile stop ... the station has only one platform, in the Austerlitz direction. The other track climbs through the station and you will see humming trains running at top notch passing through the station on their way to Porte d'Auteuil. You will not be disappointed by the sight, which is rather fascinating.' Here his friend inserts a parenthesis: 'It is horrific and not to be missed. BJP.'

Michel-Ange Auteuil station on the Line 10 loop is a ten-minute walk from the Castel Béranger, the apartment block designed by Hector Guimard that caught the eye of Adrien Bénard, President of the CMP, and inspired him (I think 'inspired' is the right word here) to give Guimard the station entrance commission. One rainy autumnal afternoon, I stepped out of Michel-Ange Auteuil to make the pilgrimage for myself.

The Castel stands on rue de la Fontaine, which today is about as grand and patrician as a suburban street can be. (I found myself walking past antique shops, stylish boulangeries and the quaint premises of a cobbler who seemed to specialise in the repair of expensive carpet slippers.) But during the Belle

Époque, rue de la Fontaine was a testing ground for progressive Art Nouveau architecture. There's a sinuosity to the tall, pale apartment blocks, and Guimard designed several of them. His masterpiece stands out, though, as the culmination of the wildness that has been brewing along the street. The Castel reminded me of the way a normal building would be depicted in a cartoon if shown through the eyes of a drunk. The essential structure seemed like several disparate Gothic towers shoved together, and this was offset by many swirling decorations around windows and balconies in green steel and stone. The green and orange metal front gate was a scribble of whiplash curves. I could imagine that Guimard's Metro triffids had come marching or oozing out of here to take Paris by storm.

As I photographed the building, the gate clanged open and a small elderly woman in dark glasses stepped out. It slowly occurred to me that she was one of the best-dressed people I had ever seen. Her jacket and skirt looked misshapen at first (until I thought about it), and all her colours ought not to have matched – green and blue, red and orange (the latter provided by the strap of her handbag) – but they did. She hurried away when she saw me, presumably because she was famous (a person dressed like that could not have remained obscure) and didn't want to be photographed. Her stylishness, of course, was a posthumous compliment to Guimard, since she had chosen to live in his building.

I did wonder if she was heading off to the Metro, which must be a home-from-home for her.

Line 11

Being a latecomer, Line 11 was blessedly free of entanglements
arising from that pipe dream of an inner circle. It opened in
1935, from Châtelet (crux of the Grande Croisée) to our old
stomping ground, Porte des Lilas. In 1937, it was extended by
one stop beyond Porte des Lilas to Mairie des Lilas, and that's
it for *now*. A big future awaits Line 11, however, and we will be
coming to that.

Line 11 is like the single hand of a clock, pointing towards
two. It'd probably be quite tedious to be a driver on the present
Line 11, because it only takes fifteen minutes to travel the whole
length and it's all underground. Then again, things might
be enlivened by the steep subterranean gradient up towards
Belleville. Clive Lamming calls Line 11 'the most unusual line
of the Metro', with 'continuous ramps more worthy of a moun-
tain railway', and indeed the middle section of the line, between
République and Belleville, was conceived as a replacement for
the Belleville funicular, one of the first projects of Fulgence
Bienvenüe, which had been decommissioned in 1924.

(Paris retains another funicular: the Montmartre Funicular,
which is not in fact a funicular because the up and down cars
are not counterbalanced, but independently electrified and
thoroughly modern-looking. It's operated by RATP, and Metro
tickets can be used for the ride, the nearest stations being Anvers
on Line 2 and Abbesses on 12. An earlier incarnation of the
Montmartre Funicular is shown in the opening sequence of

Jean-Pierre Melville's film, *Bob Le Flambeur*, accompanied by a commentary about how there is heaven and hell in Montmartre: the montage of shots suggests that heaven is Sacré-Coeur, hell is Pigalle, and the funicular is the conduit, or limbo, between them.)

The hilliness of Line 11 explains the name of Télégraphe station, the stop before Porte des Lilas. In his *Paris Dreambook*, Lawrence Osborne calls this the most 'mysterious' Metro name, but it's not so mysterious if you remember that 'telegraph' means far-writing, and then get out at Télégraphe and look. You're at the top of the hill, the highest point in Paris – as well as being opposite Belleville Cemetery – and it's often blowy up there. In 1793 Claude Chappe, developer of the first viable semaphore system, conveyed a message from this hill to St Martin-du-Tertre, 35 kilometres away, using a device with moving wooden arms, and resembling a very involved railway signal placed at the top of a tower. His signalling machine was located on a spot just beyond the cemetery, where two water towers now stand. You couldn't do semaphore from there today – too many blocks of flats in the way – so perhaps the station name is mysterious after all, partly for that reason and partly for its elision of two communication modes: train and telegraph. I trust that April Fool's Day substitution of the station name by '#TWEET' is now a little more explicable.

The station is the starting point for the compelling chase sequence in *Le Samouraï*, which is mainly a Line 11 affair. There is no classic vault at Télégraphe, which has one of those strengthening walls, but it does have white tiles, and it's among those stations where the CMP emulated Nord-Sud grandeur, so the name is written big in tiles, white on blue, and the honey-coloured poster frames are ornate. The main thing is the whiteness, though, because this is a deliberately washed-out-looking film.

My friend Julian Pepinster suggested that Jean-Pierre Melville, director of *Le Samouraï*, might have been attracted to Line 11 for another reason. Its trains were the latest thing in *matériel pneu*, the MP55s, whereas today, it has MP59s, which are the oldest trains on the network and will be replaced by new MP trains when the line extension opens. Both stocks have *loqueteaux*, and Alain Delon, playing the film's assassin-hero, Jef (a minimalistic name for a minimalistic film), makes expert use of one to quit the train at the last moment, at Jourdain, having worked out that the woman who has just climbed aboard is – even though she looks like Miss Marple – a policewoman who is tailing him while keeping in touch with police headquarters by radio.

Jef then doubles back east on Line 11, changing at Place des Fêtes onto the 7*bis* loop, although 7*bis* hadn't been designated separately from Line 7 when the film was shot. By now another, younger policewoman is tailing Jef, as he is well aware. We don't see him going around the loop, but we know he is, because the copper leading the chase is watching his progress on a giant Metro map – like a larger version of a PILI map – and as the policewoman tailing Jef passes through them the stations light up.

Having gone round the loop, Jef sticks with Line 7 as he rides back west into the middle of town, finally shaking off his tail at Châtelet, which he does by jumping off one of the two moving walkways there and simply running away. I have read that this is the same walkway along which Jules, hero of *Diva*, rides his moped in a Metro chase fifteen years later. I believe the walls on either side of the two moving walkways at Châtelet have changed colour several times. Anyhow, the walls featured in *Le Samouraï* are white; in *Diva*, they're red, as demanded by the films' differing colour palettes.

Being a late arrival, Line 11 went underneath other lines and, since its stations lay deep, they were all equipped with escalators, a rare commodity at the time on the generally shallow Metro, even though the world's first one had been demonstrated at the Paris Exposition of 1900, and the Metro got its first (Père Lachaise, 1909) two years before the London Underground (Earl's Court, 1911). By 1932 there were still only thirty-two escalators on the Metro. The rule, after the Second World War, was that one should only be provided if *voyageurs* had to ascend more than 12 metres, a cannily chosen target, since the climb at many stations was just a little short of that. By 1967, there were eighty-seven escalators – a not-very-impressive figure, given that there were often two at the same station. The development of the RER network, whose stations were plentifully supplied with escalators, guilt-tripped the RATP into action on the Metro, which now has about 500. But lifts remain rare. Only Line 14, which has a lift at every station as well as escalators, is step-free. The Grand Paris Express will be, too.

My Francophobe friend would see this shortfall as a good

example of French heartlessness: 'French motorists won't pull over for an ambulance, you know?' he once informed me, in his confiding way. If that's true (which I doubt), it might be because French ambulances, with their oddly fey sirens, are too quiet, as against British ones, which are too loud. (Their horrible screams must have caused a lot of cardiac emergencies necessitating the summoning of an ambulance.)

The fact is there aren't many lifts on the Metro because the stations are too shallow to accommodate them, and usually there's no surface building to house the lift gear. I admit, however, that there is slightly less cosseting of passengers on French railways in general than on British ones. Unlike in Britain, for example, the lines are not fenced, and there remain plenty of public crossings where you simply walk across boards placed between the tracks. My friend the railway consultant says that French railway engineers 'are sometimes surprised at how heavily signalled and interlocked everything is on British railways'. He thinks this is because French railways have usually been state-controlled, 'and the state can do what it wants'. But I don't think the Metro is heartless. For instance, some of the lines do have suicide pits (which are also on some Underground lines) into which somebody throwing themselves in front of a train might fall, so that the train goes over rather than into them. And surely the Metro term for suicides – *'accident grave de voyageur'* – is less brutal than the London equivalent: 'a person under a train'?

One contributor to an online forum discussing the accessibility of Metro stations notes that Parisian buses are now step-free, adding, 'Buses will take you everywhere, and probably with a better class of passenger, too.' But climbing stairs is a Parisian trope, an aspect of the city's romance. For the soundtrack of his film *French Cancan* (1955) Jean Renoir wrote the lyrics of a song called 'La Complainte de la Butte', which describes the stairs up the hill as 'painful' to the working-class inhabitants.

One of the most frequently photographed station entrances is that of Lamarck-Caulaincourt on Line 12, which is flanked by steps leading up Montmartre hill, so giving the impression of the station as something below stairs, like a coal hole. And having climbed the steps out of their local Metro, Parisians do the same when they reach their seven-storey Haussmann block, which is perhaps one reason why they are usually thin. 'In France, walking up and down stairs is part of everyone's day', wrote Mirielle Guiliano in *Why French Women Don't Get Fat*, and in Paris, she added, people often have no choice, 'the city being full of old buildings without lifts'. A friend of mine who works in publishing reports that, having read that, some women stopped using the lift at 20 Vauxhall Bridge Road, home of Guiliano's UK publisher. (I think that, instead of having signs warning people against climbing the stairs at deep Tube stations, there should be signs reading: 'Do consider climbing these stairs. It might be good for you.')

On YouTube there's a short film called 'The Escalator, Madeleine Metro', posted and filmed by Richard Wexler. It shows two flights of double escalators operatically arranged, and mellowly lit by a golden light, in such a way that the rising steps are reflected in the adjacent glass panels, creating a dreamy disorientation. Wexler shot the film in 2011. In a comment below, he records that he returned to Madeleine in 2015, and the effect had been lost: 'Someone turned up the lights.'

There's a particularly long escalator (for the Metro) at Télégraphe, and to the British *voyageur* it seems interestingly bleak and bereft: there are no posters to look at as you ascend or descend, only a thin line of brown tiles on each of the two white walls, reflecting the fact that, on the Metro, escalators have traditionally been an afterthought, not quite bedded into the system.

And now for that big – and step-free – future.

Line 11 is to be extended by half a dozen stops, from Mairie des Lilas to Rosny-Bois-Perrier, where it will meet Line 15 of the Grand Paris Express. There will be an elevated section on the way, the first Metro viaduct for more than forty years. The first station after Mairie des Lilas on the extension will be called Serge Gainsbourg, in recognition, no doubt, of his whole cultural contribution and not just that song about the ticket puncher at the line's original terminus. Given Gainsbourg's reputation as decadent, this seems akin to a London Underground station being called Keith Richards.

Lines 12, 13 and the first Line 14

Line 12 is a soothing, relatively quiet line, with elderly trains (MF67s) and the reassuring line colour of 'fir tree'. It seems to take its users not only across Paris in a north–south trajectory, but also back in time to a more refined past.

Line 12 is most at home when it passes through the 7th Arrondissement, where my wife Lisa and I sometimes stay in a small, somnolent hotel behind the Musée d'Orsay. What with the presence of the museum and the National Assembly, the 7th is dignified and patrician, although in *Paris Revealed* Stephen Clarke puts it differently: 'The people there are posh and they know it.'

On those occasions, Solférino is our home station and, early on a Saturday evening, it's nice to know it's waiting there, with its restful adjacent garden and beautiful platform tiling, as we prepare to travel south on Line 12 towards Notre-Dame-des-Champs, from where we will walk to that festive, gilded brasserie, La Coupole (which is not as expensive as you might think).

We prepare for that Metro ride in our distinct ways: Lisa takes a long bath, while I (having taken a *short* bath) have an aperitif in one of the nearby bars and, the 7th being so dignified, these are usually located within restaurants that do not seek the raucous Saturday night crowds, so the chairs are being put on the tables around me as I sip my glass of white and read my novel. This is done politely, I should add, and not in my immediate vicinity, and I enjoy knowing that, as Saturday evening comes to a premature end in the 7th, it will be only just beginning at La Coupole in the 14th.

*

Line 12 is attractive because it was built by the only rival to the CMP (Paris being spared the free-for-all of London Tube building), the Société du Chemin de Fer Électrique Souterrain Nord-Sud de Paris. The Nord-Sud – which would create two lines: today's 12 and the north part of 13 – was founded in 1904 by Jean-Baptiste Berlier, who goes down as one of the great railway romantics, that class of people whose schemes were more graceful than profitable. Among their number I would include Isambard Kingdom Brunel, who stuck with his 7-foot track gauge, which gave a fast and smooth ride, long after it was clear that the rest of Britain was going with niggardly 4 foot 8½, and a flamboyant American, James Sherwood, whose company, Great North Eastern Railway, ran the East Coast Main-line in Britain from 1996 to 2007, using stylishly fitted-out trains equipped with dining cars. (He also founded the Venice Simplon Orient Express, which *is* profitable – or should be, given the price of the tickets.)

Line 12 began life as the Nord-Sud's Line A (the CMP having the exclusive right to use numbers). It opened in stages from 1910, and by 1916 it ran from Porte de la Chapelle on the North Bank to Porte de Versailles on the South.

I have mentioned how the Nord-Sud lines had higher vaults than those of the CMP; how the white bevelled tiles they had in common with CMP stations were embellished with coloured ceramics forming swag patterns on the station walls, bands going over the vault and borders to the poster frames, at the corners of which the letters N and S are intertwined in ceramic relief, as though having sex. The embellishing tiles (which also appeared as bands running at eye level in the corridors, giving *voyageurs* a preview of what was to come) were brown in ordinary stations served by a single line, green for junctions and termini – and one station, Madeleine on Line 12, had blue tiles (surviving in a corridor but removed from the platform by subsequent refurbishment) for no known reason. Perhaps someone had a blue-eyed girlfriend called Madeleine.

As on the CMP, station names were written in white on blue, but the Nord-Sud always wrote them in ceramics (sometimes the early CMP names had been written on paper; later, enamel was used). The letters spelling out the names might be a metre or more tall, so when Lines A and B opened in 1910 and 1911 there could be no doubt where you were (providing you could read). On the tunnel headwalls of the former Line A, 'Montmartre' and 'Montparnasse' are romantically inscribed in Art Nouveau lettering at the north and south ends respectively, with a delicate flighted arrow, depicted at a falling-from-the-sky angle, showing the platform you need for each.

The tunnels so inscribed were photographed in early 1910, prior to the opening of the line, when Paris was flooded by the rising waters of the Seine after weeks of heavy rain. 'The Seine rose to such heights,' writes Tamara Hovey in *Paris Underground*, 'that it rippled around the tip of the beard of the Zouave soldier on the Alma Bridge.'

The great flood rather suited Line A. The photographs show scenes of an almost Venetian elegance with men sitting in rowing boats in the stations, and the directions written on the tunnel headwalls still apply – it's just that you'd have to *row* your way to Montmartre or Montparnasse. (All the subterranean Metro lines were flooded in 1910; indeed, they acted as drains, drawing water off the streets.)

In Nord-Sud stations outside central Paris, 'Porte de la Chapelle' and 'Porte de Versailles' are written on the headwalls, and if those two places are not quite as romantic as the other two, the Nord-Sud tried to make them so with the palatial stations it built there. (On the former Line B, the tunnel headwalls proclaimed 'Clichy Saint-Ouen' and 'Saint-Lazare'.)

In December 1929, the Nord-Sud opened a new Porte de Versailles station on Line A, 100 metres south of the previous one, and you can see the ghost of the old vault as you approach the 'new' one. This was done as part of the line's proposed extension further south to Mairie d'Issy, to serve a new park. But it would be the CMP who built that next stretch, because on 1 January 1930 the Nord-Sud, crippled by the cost of building its lines, was taken over by it, and Line A became Line 12.

One Metro book on my shelves invites us to picture Berlier in December 1929 standing alone amid the grandeur of his just-rebuilt Porte de Versailles southern terminus at the end of the one day that station was controlled by the Nord-Sud. It's a poignant picture: the great engineer contemplating the end of his beautiful empire, and wondering why he deserved this fate, given the considerateness he showed to *voyageurs*, exemplified at Porte de Versailles by the decorative green tiles, complementing the white, and letting people know that this was a terminus, even if not for long. But Berlier died in 1911. I know that because there's a plaque commemorating him at Saint-Lazare – 'Sans Oublier Jean-Baptiste Berlier' – and it gives his dates, so the picture painted in that otherwise reliable book is surely incorrect. But if the image is illusory, it is emotionally powerful, and perhaps the author was fantasising, invoking the *ghost* of Berlier; or perhaps the author had inadvertently placed Berlier in Porte de Versailles when they really meant his architect, Lucien Bechmann, who lived until 1968.

The Nord-Sud stations are regarded as the Metro masterpieces, but we shouldn't forget that the CMP had initiated the distinguished white-vault template, and it's not as if that company – aware of being beaten at its own game – didn't learn from the rival outfit. The CMP borrowed some of the Nord-Sud tricks, so you will see station names in blue and white tiles, and ornate, coloured faience poster frames on some stations not built by the Nord-Sud, as for example those on sleepy *3bis*, where the poster frames are lovingly described as 'ochre or honey-coloured' by Daniel Wright, transport writer, author of the Beauty of Transport website. In a post of 4 December 2014 called 'When Two Tiles Go to War', Wright suggests the two companies got into an 'art race (rather than an arms race)' during the 1920s, and the CMP continued its perpetuation of Nord-Sud styles after it absorbed the company in 1930.

Reading from north to south, original Nord-Sud tiling survives on Line 12 at Porte de La Chapelle, Solférino and Pasteur, which is doubly blessed, having not only Nord-Sud ceramics but also a Guimard entrance (because it also serves the CMP's line 6), and Porte de Versailles.

Several stations on both Lines 12 and 13 have reproduction Nord-Sud tiles. On Line 12, see for example Lamarck-Caulaincourt, Sèvres Babylone and Notre-Dame-des-Champs, where, owing to the station name being written so large, it was necessary to render it as N-D DES CHAMPS, with a tiny 'DES' (otherwise it would have been even larger). We must be grateful for the reproductions; they put to shame those Line 12 stations stuck with inept facelifts, for example Pigalle, with its big, boring, flat white tiles; but there is for the moment a toothpaste gleam to some of the repro stations.

Nord-Sud tiling is charmingly old-fashioned, a bad look when the 1960s rolled around, which explains why its ceramics were especially likely to be subjected to *carrossage*, or 'covering', the first departure from white-vault purity. When I visited Marx Dormoy station on Line 12, the *carrossage* was being removed, disclosing the original tiling, which was brown and white, Marx Dormoy being neither a junction nor a terminus – the humblest sort of station, therefore. Even so, the tiling was impressive. No workmen were present at the time of my visit, but I thought of them as archaeologists rather than builders.

My favourite Line 12 station – and perhaps on the whole Metro – is Porte de la Chapelle, which was the line's northern terminus (hence green tiles in addition to the white) for nearly a hundred years. The station retains a perfect vault, albeit a wider one than usual, since it accommodates three tracks and two island platforms. My allegiance to it owes something to the fact that, on the two occasions I've been there, I've had the place to myself, and my loneliness was emphasised by the size of the station, the size of the letters proclaiming the station name, and by the works of art that have displaced advertisements in those large poster frames, and which depict similarly depopulated Metro scenes. I can never tell whether Porte de la Chapelle is overlit or underlit. The brightness of the fluorescent lights, held in basic steel fittings, such as you might see in a factory, seems to falter at the top of the vault, allowing that familiar Metro station shimmer to become almost glittering. I have never got out at Porte de La Chapelle, which graces a relatively poor part of Paris.

Often cited as Lucien Bechmann's greatest gift to Paris is the subterranean circular ticket hall at Saint-Lazare, created to allow passenger transfers between Nord-Sud's A and B Lines, and used as a meeting place by Parisians just as Piccadilly Circus is by Londoners. Here is Daniel Wright again, from a piece called 'When Two Tiles Go to War':

Clad in ceramic tiles, columns with sort-of-Corinthian leafy capitals support a groin-vaulted roof over the circular ticket hall. The tiling on the columns is quite outstanding. Rectangular white tiles run vertically, separated by smaller orange-brown mosaic tiles, while the white tiles at the top of the columns are decorated with stylised green flowers. There are also (and why not?) small green ceramic studs placed around the columns. Uplighters in the capitals bounce light off the reflective tiles which cover the whole of the ceiling. If you're not expecting it, coming across the rotunda is absolutely breathtaking.

In *Nairn's Paris*, Ian Nairn described the ticket hall as 'a whirling Art Nouveau arabesque without a single decorative trick to it; everything is done by shape and style'. Nairn prefers it to Piccadilly Circus, built nearly twenty years later. I myself like Piccadilly Circus, but its glamour comes from its soft, golden glow: the expensive marble and hardwood fittings, its kiosk-like shops, giving the air of a West End street at night, and the World Clock, from which you can tell the time anywhere in the world (when it's working) – Piccadilly Circus being the centre of the world, from a British perspective. But as a rotunda, the station of that name seems stiff and barrel-like compared to Bechmann's work at Saint-Lazare.

In 2012, Line 12 breached the *northern* city boundary with an extension to working-class (as its name implies) Aubervilliers Front Populaire. In 2022, the line was extended further north to Mairie d'Aubervilliers (a distance of 1.4 kilometres, all in tunnel). I visited this station in summer 2020, a few weeks after it opened. It is very large and white, with much pale wood and steel, and light fittings in the form of wide, white illuminated circles, like the floating haloes of saints. There was no station vault, but perhaps, in view of the general lightness, none was needed. I sensed that a new Metro template was being created,

and indeed Mairie D'Aubervilliers is where Line 12 will inter-
sect with Line 15 of the Grand Paris Express.

Today's Line 13 started life as Nord-Sud's Line B. It began in
1911, running north from Saint-Lazare to Porte de Saint-Ouen,
and until 1973 it was an entirely North Bank phenomenon.

Its northern half, having being built by the Nord-Sud company, is more beautiful than its southern half, so Line 13 is like
a man wearing a tailored vintage jacket, but with trousers from
Marks & Spencer's lounge suit range.

In 1912, a branch was created on this stretch. As we have
seen, branches are considered heretical on the Metro – this one
especially so because, unlike most, it's not at the end of a line
but occurs at a central point, a deep wound, undermining Line
13's aesthetic Nord-Sud appeal.

The branch was opened from La Fourche (three stops north
of Saint-Lazare) to Porte de Clichy, a north-westerly trajectory, and we will refer to the two prongs thus created as the
Saint-Ouen and Clichy branches, even though they've since
been extended beyond those early termini. La Fourche means
'fork', and that's what it is. It's also a bottleneck for relatively
less well-off commuters heading away from or towards Paris's
busiest main-line station, Saint-Lazare.

It's impressive to read that uningratiating station name
outlined in brown in the large Nord-Sud format, this being a
junction; but anyone pointing out the beauty of the ceramics
here at rush hour would be thought deranged. La Fourche, and

the other two stations feeding in and out of Saint-Lazare from the north (Liège and Place de Clichy), have barriers between the trains and the platforms not because the trains are automatic (the usual reason for barriers), but to stop *voyageurs* from being bustled onto the tracks, such is the press of people, and high-vis-wearing RATP staffers are also on hand to marshal the crowds. It seems wrong to apply the romantic term '*voyageurs*' to the riders on peak-hour Line 13 hereabouts. La Fourche in particular, which is subject to the churn of people changing trains for the branch they want, is the veritable armpit of the Metro, epitomising – and perhaps justifying – the cynical Parisian jingle, '*Metro, Boulot, Dodo*'.

Adding to the great headache of La Fourche is the fact that it's two stations, one below the other. In English you'd call them La Fourche Upper and La Fourche Lower, but it sounds better in French: La Fourche Supérieure and La Fourche Inférieure. The former has the classic vault, two tracks and platforms and reproduction tiles; the latter has original tiles and is half the size, like the child of the upper station: it has one side platform and one track and is served only by trains heading towards Saint-Lazare from the Porte de Saint-Ouen branch.

A word about the station two stops south of La Fourche, Liège.

It's arguably the most beautiful Metro station – an art gallery in a site of commuter trauma. First, it has original Nord-Sud tiles. Secondly, instead of adverts for Vodafone or whatever, the poster frames contain moody ceramic depictions of the Belgian city of Liège, after which the station is named.

Thirdly, the station is offset, owing to the narrowness of the streets above. That's to say, there are in effect two stations, each with a perfectly parabolical vault and two tracks, but only one platform. You go past the 'first' Liège, with the single platform, glorious tiles and paintings on one side; then you go past the 'second' with the whole cornucopia on the other side, and I'm sure most tourists don't rationalise the situation, especially if they've been caught up in a peak hour crowd. They probably just write the flickering moment off as a case of déja-vu, tiredness or incipient brain degeneration.

At the CMP takeover of the Nord-Sud in 1930, Line B became Line 13, although some Parisians still speak of the 'Nord-Sud lines'.

What the Nord-Sud had planned as Line C was opened by the CMP in 1937 as Line 14, the first of two lines to carry that number. It ran across the South Bank from Invalides down to Porte de Vanves. Between 1973 and 1976, Line 13 (entirely on the North Bank) was linked to this original Line 14 (entirely on the South Bank) by an under-river tunnel; it was also extended north and south. This bolted-together line was designated Line 13 and the name Line 14 disappeared, only to be used again in 1998 for *today's* Line 14.

In 1980, the north-west-pointing Clichy branch was extended to Gabriel Péri, by which it crosses over the serpentine Seine, which recurs west of Paris, probably to the surprise of many tourists, since this part of the river does not usually feature on the Metro maps – and so a *pleasant* surprise. This is the stretch of the Seine depicted by George Seurat in his pointillist masterpieces, 'A Sunday Afternoon on the Island of La Grande Jatte' and 'Bathers at Asnières' (whose central figure, the gormless boy sitting on the riverbank, looks like Boris Johnson). You can tell from the latter that this is not the Seine of central Paris familiar to tourists, because there are hazy factory chimneys in the background. Today, the view is of the towers of La Défense to the left as you head away from town, and building sites all around, but there are also plenty of trees and a line of picturesque, old-fashioned boats moored near the viaduct that carries the line. In 2008, this branch was extended again, via Les Agnettes (where it will receive Line 15 of the Grand Paris Express) to the preposterously named Asnières-Gennevilliers Les Courtilles.

In 1998, the Saint-Ouen branch extended further north to Saint-Denis Université, to serve that popular institution. The new Metro is paying a lot of attention to Seine-Saint-Denis, poorest *département* of the Petit-Couronne, and the main hub of the Grand Paris Express project will be located there when Line 14 is extended to a new showpiece station, Saint-Denis Pleyel.

I have perhaps been too dismissive of the stations at the south end of Line 13. The best of them show the CMP's genuflection to Nord-Sud style: station names in blue and white ceramics, moderately elaborate poster frames. See for example Gaîté, in Montparnasse, whose nomenclature is interesting. It's named after rue de la Gaîté, a road leading up the Wall of the Farmers General where a tax on wine (among other goods entering Paris) was imposed. Restaurants, theatres and places of jollification were set up outside the walls before the high prices kicked in. Rue de la Gaîté remains, according to the Paris Tourist Office website (en.parisinfo.com), 'a lively street full of cafés and restaurants' and 'home to a number of performing arts venues since the nineteenth century ... This is definitely the place to check out for an evening's entertainment.' Until recently, it also used to be full of sex shops, which either did or did not undermine the station's name, depending on your point of view, but what surely does undermine it is the direct proximity of Montparnasse Cemetery. Ever since the station was opened in 1937, Parisian mourners must have been convening at a station called (to translate) 'Gaiety'.

In 2021, the station gained the subtitle 'Josephine Baker', to mark the fact that her last performance had been at a theatre called Bobino on rue de la Gaîté – and Bobino survives there as a performance space. Josephine Baker might be thought of as justifying the good-time vibe of the station name, but there was more to her than that: she was also a decorated hero of the French Resistance.

The Second Line 14

The second Line 14 would be the first new Metro line since the opening of Line 11 in 1935, and it's the spoilt youngest child of the family, showcase and showpiece of the network. The stations look like sets for a science fiction film, and this was reflected in the acronymic nickname given to the line when it was in development: Météor (Metro Est–Ouest Rapide), which also nods to the speed of its automatic trains, and the approximate line direction.

Line 14 lies deep for a Metro line, and, like the London Tube, it was excavated using tunnelling shields, albeit with two-track tunnels. It opened in 1998, from Madeleine on the North Bank, where its line colour – hoity-toity iris – joined the accumulating rainbow of lines (Line 1, and RER A and D) following the diagonal of the river down through central Paris, taking in Châtelet and Gare de Lyon. It then turned sharp right under the river to Bibliothèque François Mitterrand, flagship of the 'Paris Rive Gauche' regeneration of the Austerlitz railway lands. As well as relieving Line 1, the purpose of Line 14 was to embrace the formerly industrial districts of east Paris, and in this sense it's the equivalent of the equally spectacular Jubilee Line Extension in London.

Line 14 goes under the river, but it was originally planned to go over, and the bridge designer would have had the challenge of competing with Viaduc d'Austerlitz, which carries Line 5 hereabouts, and Pont de Passy, which carries Line 6, but budgetary constraints intervened. They also scotched another early plan – for the creation of great wells along the line, to admit daylight to the stations.

In 2003, Line 14 was extended north by one stop from Madeleine to Saint-Lazare; in 2007, it was extended by one stop at the other end to Olympiades, a zone of high-concept high-rises poorly connected to the middle of town. In 2020, it was extended again at the northern end, by four stops to Mairie de Saint-Ouen. Part of the plan here was to relieve congestion on Line 13 north of Saint-Lazare, but I have travelled on the supposedly relieved part of Line 13 since the opening of the Line 14 extension, and I don't see how the platforms or trains could ever have been more crowded.

The stretch from Châtelet Les Halles to Gare de Lyon is 2.78km, the longest on the Metro, and just about bearable even when the train is so crowded you can hardly move, because Line 14 trains average 40 kilometres per hour, as against 25 kph on the other lines. (The trains need to be fast – or you could say they are *enabled* to be fast – because the average distance between Line 14 stops is 2 kilometres, compared to 500 metres on the rest of the network.) The trains were the first on the Metro to be fully automatic – that is, no drivers. Where Line 14 leads, the others follow, and Lines 1 and 4 are now also driverless. 'Most of all, the rider can marvel at its *driverless mechanism*,' writes Tom Conley, in his afterword to *In the Metro* by Marc Augé, of a driverless train of Line 14 (which hadn't existed in 1986 when Augé wrote his original meditation): 'the ultimate solution of the Cartesian machinery of a soul or a driver in the cockpit of a bodily wagon or nacelle. The new train would be the metro etherealised, a utopian dream of the mechanical bent of French ingenuity' ... which is a very French way of putting it, even though Conley is American. ('Nacelle', incidentally, means the streamlined casing of car or plane.)

And RATP keeps throwing new trains at Line 14: the MP 89s were succeeded by the MP05s, then the MP14s. That they are all rubber-tyred is an endorsement of technology that some were beginning to regard as having had its day, an eccentric novelty.

The stations are big: 'future-proofed'. At Bibliothèque François Mitterrand the steps to the exit are as wide as a football terrace. At Gare de Lyon there is a tropical garden behind a glass screen adjacent to the platform, and this is watered, apparently, by 'regular thunderstorms'. I've never seen one of these, and to me the garden looks dusty and neglected – like a zoo enclosure from which the animals have escaped – but I think it is intended not so much as a botanical display as proof of spare capacity. Look, RATP seems to be saying, we even have room for a garden at this station. Another way of making the same point, with the same vaguely ecological overtone, would have been to install an aquarium. (After all, there's one on the Marseilles Metro, at Vieux Port station.)

The absence of those light wells notwithstanding, the philosophy of Line 14 was that the stations be light and open rather than warren-like. The watchword of the promotional literature was 'transparency', as against 'anxiogenic' (anxiety-making) claustrophobia. A similar philosophy dictated the large scale of the Jubilee Line Extension. But the corrective was more necessary on the deep and labyrinthine Underground than on the Metro.

Line 14 is no doubt beginning to sound un-Metro-like, what with the deep tunnels, fast trains, gigantic stations. It also seems to lack the warm, sickly-sweet Metro aroma, possibly because the platforms are not bitumised, therefore not waxed with fragrant Eau de Madeleine. Instead, the platforms are made up of light-coloured tiles. Line 14 stations do retain the characteristic Metro pallor, whether expressed in steel, stone or polished concrete, and most of them are vaulted. See Pyramides and Saint-Lazare, where the tall vaults are clad in large white tiles. (Line 14 Gare de Lyon is *not* vaulted, but then neither is Line 1 Gare de Lyon.) The pleasing curves of the vaults are echoed by the steel hoops arising from the Plexiglass platform doors that protect passengers from arriving trains.

On the latest Line 14 trains, the MP14s (variants of which are going to replace the ancient MP59s on Line 11), some seats are transverse, and cosily arranged facing each other to form alcoves, which is a retro touch, as are the colours of those seats: orange and grey, a combination I've been fond of ever since I saw it used on the French electric locomotives of the 1970s, the BB22200s, nicknamed '*nez cassé*' or 'broken nose' because they have indented fronts, which makes them look like letter Zs on the move. (I now often wear grey and orange and, if complimented on my look, I like mentioning that it's inspired by a locomotive.) Another retro feature is making a comeback on Line 14: wooden benches, albeit handsomely subdivided by armrests of dark green metal, to deter any tramps looking for a lie-down. It's starting to occur to me that there's a whimsical little film to be made about a tramp looking for a snooze on the Metro. But it's hard to imagine even one such person among 50,000 daily users of impeccable

Line 14, who are propelled at such speed not only between stations, but also into the future.

We are entering the world of the Grand Paris Express, or the Metro hereafter. This is essentially an orbital railway operating outside Paris proper, but insofar as it has a root (or route) in Paris itself, then Line 14 is it, although the extension to Line 11 is also considered part of the GPE.

Line 14 is being extended south by seven stops from Olympiades to Orly Airport. On the way, it will connect with the Villejuif branch of Line 7, at a new station that will also be served by the Grand Paris Express. Line 14 is also being extended north by one stop to a new station called Saint-Denis Pleyel, which will be the lynchpin of the Grand Paris Express. Here, the principal circle of the project, Line 15, will connect not only with Line 14 but also with the outer circles formed by Line 16 to the east and Line 18 to the west. As for Line 17, that will be essentially radial, heading north-east up to Charles de Gaulle Airport, but the GPE is about circularity. 'In Paris, they do love their circles,' the consultant engineer I have frequently consulted in the writing of this book told me, meaning the Metro engineers rather than the entire populace.

Saint-Denis Pleyel will be one of nine 'Gares Emblématiques' or showpiece stations of the GPE, each designed by a different architect. As created by Kengo Kuma (cited by *Time* magazine in 2021 as the world's most influential architect), Saint-Denis Pleyel will have nine levels flowing into one another in gentle cascades and involving much whiteness and wood, Kuma being particularly attached to that material. There is this from the website of Kengo Kuma and Associates: 'Through a multi-sensory sequence of spaces, stressful daily metropolitan movements will be changed to an open and interactive experience. From this project, the station will be a new centre of the city, and its complementary program will bring about a dynamic social and cultural dimension to the district of Pleyel.' The station will incorporate an artwork created by the Belgian musician, rapper and clothes designer Stromae (Paul Van Haver), and when the station opens in 2024, the new age of the Paris Metro will have dawned.

Au Revoir, Voyageur

In France, they do like their projects 'grand', and any account of the Grand Paris Express will be a list of superlatives. As I write, thirty TBMs (tunnel-boring machines) are creating a twenty-four-hour driverless railway of 200 kilometres' total length, serving sixty-eight new Metro stations. In other words, the kilometrage of the Metro will almost double, and the number of stations will increase by nearly a quarter, and each of those stations will be a community hub, and the generator of new housing. It is the largest infrastructure project in Western Europe. In the *Financial Times Magazine* on 14 March 2020, Simon Kuper wrote that it will bring about an urban transformation 'arguably bigger than Haussmann's in the 1850s'. It will also be beautiful, of course, and the commissioning of Stromae at Saint-Denis Pleyel might be compared to the enlistment of Guimard and his iron flowers in 1900, not least because it might be just as controversial – and controversy is free publicity, as Adrien Bénard, President of the CMP, calculated when he employed Guimard.

The Grand Paris Express will also be virtuous. It perpetuates the Paris Mayor, Anne Hidalgo's aim of weaning Paris off the automobile, and 2030, the target date for completion of the GPE, is also when combustion-fired cars are due to be banned in Paris. The GPE will also foster a reconciliation between Paris and its suburbs, but, being a foreigner, I should probably stop going on about that: it feels too much like butting in on a family quarrel.

That the new railway is being labelled as part of the Metro is a compliment to the Metro, but will it look like part of the Metro? Its trains will be bigger than Metro trains; they will go faster than all Metro trains except those on Line 14. The stations will on average be 3 kilometres apart, as against 500 metres for the Metro up to now. The Grand Paris Express lines will be both underground and overground, but so are those of the existing Metro.

I will be nearly seventy when the project is fully realised. I hope to be there at the time, and if my knees (or whatever) have gone by then, I ought to be all right because all stations will be fully accessible. Any reader suspecting an onset of sentimentality is, I'm afraid, correct. I am going to take a walk down memory lane, but it will be a short one, I promise.

Here, from a volume called *Baudelaire in English*, is a translation by F. P. Sturm of part of 'The Swan', from Charles Baudelaire's long poem, *'Les Fleurs du Mal'*, published in 1861, when Baron Haussmann was well into his purgation of the old, cluttered and shambolic Paris:

– Old Paris is no more (a town, alas,
Changes more quickly than man's heart may change)
Yet in my mind I still can see the booths;
The heaps of brick and rough-hewn capitals
The grass; the stones all over-green with moss;
The débris, and the square-set heaps of tiles.

In those lines, Baudelaire refutes the optimism of the Haussmann project. It created a cityscape that millions would come to regard as ideal, but Paris, like most places, is seen through a nostalgic lens by most people. In that book review in which Richard Cobb pursues the theme of 'Paris assassinated', he describes the disappearance of any *'esprit de quartier'*, of 'taxi drivers, typists and white-collar workers' from the 5th and 6th Arrondissements where I stayed when making my Metro pilgrimages, and which I considered bohemian and characterful even at the turn at the turn of the twentieth and twenty-first centuries.

Surely Polly Magoo, the dark and very nocturnal bar on rue du Petit Pont, where I used to drink after taking the last Metro back to my Left Bank comfort zone, retained the 'warmth and originality' Cobb claims has disappeared? And the dusty, book-lined sleeping alcoves (known as the Tumbleweed Hotel) above the fabled bookshop, Shakespeare and Co., just around the corner, still provide a refuge for would-be Baudelaires.

Admittedly, this is not the first Shakespeare and Co.: the one on rue de l'Odéon run by Sylvia Beach, who published *Ulysses*. But the man who founded the 'new' Shakespeare & Co., George

Whitman, still embodied Left Bank bohemianism despite being (or precisely because he was) an exile from Boston, America. I had a long conversation with Whitman, a small, tousled, mischievous man in battered corduroy, in the fiftieth-anniversary year of his shop's opening in 1951; he was eighty-eight at the time. As we spoke, the shop phone was ringing: 'We never answer the phone,' he drawled. Regarding criteria for admission to the 'Tumbleweed Hotel', Whitman (once known as 'the Don Quixote of the Latin Quarter') said, 'We always take a chance on a pretty girl.' Yes, the 6th Arrondissement had been different when he arrived: 'This area was a slum, with dingy hotels, wine shops, little laundries, needle-and-thread shops.' But Whitman had not capitulated to bland corporatism.

My Paris routine was to buy a book from Shakespeare & Co. on the evening before my return to London. I would begin reading the book in Polidor, that quaint bistro on rue Monsieur le Prince frequented by Ernest Hemingway, where you sit at long, communal tables, and some of my fellow diners obviously disapproved of my reading (in Paris, you're supposed to concentrate on the *food*). The next morning – to gloss over the various bars that intervened after Polidor – I would carry on with the book as I rode the Line 4 Metro train back to Gare du Nord. The Metro ticket would be my bookmark as I continued to read on the Eurostar back to London, and I would retain it after I'd finished the book, a souvenir and promise of return to Paris – much like Mario's Metro ticket in *The Wages of Fear*.

After I met my wife-to-be, there were longer Parisian

intervals between my Eurostar journeys. Her flat was near the rue Mouffetard, which, according to Richard Cobb, had lost its 'intense sociability', but there seemed to me to be a constant Parisian street party going on roundabout. It's just that Cobb had been there before me. Ernest Hemingway had in turn been there before Cobb, and no doubt Hemingway – who recorded, in *A Moveable Feast*, the sight of herds of goats being driven down the street to supply milk to the locals – would have thought Cobb was experiencing a less characterful, more homogenised version of the city he lived in during the 1940s and 50s. Anyone can play at Cobb's game, albeit maybe not with his lyricism. For instance, I recall the days when the single unisex lavatory in Polidor was in traditional French style, which is to say there *was* no lavatory, merely a hole in the ground in an agricultural-looking outhouse. It was characterful, you could say.

As for the Metro, I knew the network when *voyageurs* carried cardboard tickets, unconnected to any electronic matrix; when the purity of the station vaults was not spoiled by glass screens erected along the platforms to protect people from automatic trains, because there were no automatic trains, but rather trains dating from the 1960s or even the fifties, with spartan metallic interiors and doors with *loqueteaux*, those embodiments of existential freedom, and ladders eccentrically and unashamedly displayed. This, generally speaking, is the Metro described in this book, and I like it, but that's not to say the Grand Paris Express won't be just as likely to engage people's imaginations, or that it will lack what Lawrence Osborne described as the Metro's 'innate tendency to dream'; but those dreamers will all be much younger than me and with a different Paris in their heads.

I am belatedly conscious that trying to convey my love of the Paris Metro might, to some people, seem a bizarre project. It definitely does to my Francophobe friend. 'Jesus Christ,' he said, simply, when I told him what I was about. I can imagine that, even to people less prejudiced, the Metro might be just an amenity: an efficient (and surely nobody can deny its efficiency) method of getting from A to B, and I suppose people so inclined will not have been reading this book. If they have, it's likely they would have found my evocations of the play of light on the station vaults (like so many overhead rivers), or the satisfaction of being on the elevated sections (those stately fairground rides), or the hallucinatory charm of the Guimard entrances illuminated at night (when they seem to be encouraging decadent behaviour) merely bemusing.

I can empathise with such people to the extent that I can see how the Metro might be appreciated on a more low-key level. Its trains are as swift, cosy and well targeted as taxis, and the Metro is sufficiently reliable that it will probably not ruin your day by some great seizure (which the London Underground can and will do); it gently assists one's appreciation of Paris, where there is so much to appreciate. It is like the friendly waiter who shows you to your table, brings you the menu and the water, then modestly retreats into the background, to be replaced by some more flamboyant but (in my usual experience) equally friendly character; or the barman who doesn't mind that you've made a mess yet again of pronouncing *'vin rouge'*; or the assistant at the Musée Carnavelet who smiles at your look of embarrassment at being so close to the very bed where Marcel Proust wrote his great novel.

But imagine looking again at these humble facilitators, and seeing that they are really very beautiful, as indeed they might well be, and as the Paris Metro certainly is.

By the way, as I reflect on the title of this last chapter ... *'voyageur'* does look much better than 'voyager'. I really must (to quote Clive James again) 'get enough French to travel on the Metro'.

Bibliography of Quoted Sources

Edmondo des Amicis, *Studies of Paris* (G. P. Putnam's and
  Son, 1882)
Anonymous, *Metro de Paris* (Hachette, 1969)
Michel Augé, *In The Metro* (University of Minnesota Press, 2002)
Karl Baedeker, *Paris and Its Environs* (Baedeker, 1904)
John Betjeman, *Collected Poems* (John Murray, 2006)
Benson Bobrick, *Labyrinths of Iron: Subways in History, Myth, Art
  and War* (Newsweek Books, 1981)
Gayle K. Brunelle and Annette Finley-Croswhite, *Murder in
  the Metro: Laetitia Toureaux and the Cagoule in 1930s France*
  (Louisiana State University Press, 2010)
Carol Clarke and Robert Sykes (editors), *Baudelaire in English*
  (Penguin, 1997)
Stephen Clarke, *Paris Revealed: The Secret Life of a City* (Black
  Swan, 2011)
Agatha Christie, *The Mystery of the Blue Train* (William Collins
  & Sons, 1928)

Matthew Cobb, *Resistance: The French Fight Against the Nazis* (Simon & Schuster UK, 2010)

Matthew Cobb *Eleven Days in August: The Liberation of Paris in 1944* (Simon & Schuster, 2013)

Richard Cobb, *Paris and Elsewhere: Selected Writings*, edited and introduced by David Gilmour (John Murray, 1998)

Richard Cobb, *Promenades: A Historian's Appreciation of Modern French Literature* (Oxford University Press, 1980)

Christine Colin, *Questions(s), design* (Flammarion, 2010)

Helen Constantine (translator), *Paris Metro Tales* (Oxford University Press, 2011)

Charles Dickens, *Dombey and Son* (Oxford University Press, 1974)

Norma Evenson, *Paris: A Century of Change (1878–1978)* (Yale University Press, 1979)

Christine Féret-Fleury, *The Girl Who Reads on the Metro* (Pan Books, 2017)

Carlos López Galviz, *Cities, Railways, Modernities* (Routledge, 2019)

George Gissing, *In the Year of Jubilee* (Lawrence and Bullen, 1894)

Christoph Groneck, *U-Bahn, S-Bahn and Tram in Paris: Urban Rail in the French Capital* (Schwandl, 2020)

Mireille Guiliano, *Why French Women Don't Get Fat: The Secret of Eating For Pleasure* (Vintage, 2006)

Brian Hardy, *Paris Metro Handbook* (Capital Transport, 1988)

Ernest Hemingway, *A Movable Feast* (Scribner's, 1964)

Tamara Hovey, *Paris Underground* (Orchard Books, 1991)

Andrew Hussey, *Paris: The Secret History* (Penguin, 2006)

Clive James, *Gate of Lilacs: A Verse Commentary on Proust*
(Picador, 2016)

Clive Lamming, *The Story of the Paris Metro (From 1900 to the
Present Day)* (Éditions Glénat, 2017)

Olivier de Landreville, *Les Grand Travaux de Paris*
(Baudry, 1887)

Bryan Morgan, *The End of the Line: A Book About Railways and
Places, Mainly Continental* (Cleaver-Hume Press, 1955)

Ian Nairn, *Nairn's Paris* (Penguin, 1968)

George Orwell, *Down and Out in Paris and London*
(Penguin, 1940)

Lawrence Osborne, *Paris Dreambook: An Unconventional Guide to
the Splendour and Squalor of the City* (Pantheon, 1990)

Mark Ovenden (with Peter B. Lloyd and Julian Pepinster,
editors), *Paris Metro Style (in Map and Station Design)* (Capital
Transport, 2008)

Brian Patton, *Paris RER Handbook* (Capital Transport, 2001)

B. J. Prigmore, *On Rails Under Paris* (Light Railway Transport
Press, 1970)

Marcel Proust, *Sodom and Gomorrah (In Search of Lost Time,
Volume 4)* (Penguin, 2003)

Jean Rhys, *Quartet* (Chatto and Windus, 1928)

Graham Robb, *Parisians: An Adventure History of Paris*
(Picador, 2010)

Georges Simenon, *Maigret and the Headless Corpse* (Harcourt
Brace, 1955)

Georges Simenon, *Maigret's Christmas* (Hamish
Hamilton, 1976)

Georges Simenon, *Maigret's Revolver* (Hamish Hamilton, 1956)

Georges Simenon, *The Move* (Hamish Hamilton, 1967)

Georges Simenon, *Maigret's Memoirs* (Hamish Hamilton, 1963)

Simon Webb, *Commuters: The History of a British Way of Life* (Pen and Sword, 2016)

Andrew White (editor), *The Time Out Book of Paris Walks* (Penguin, 1999)

Edmund White, *The Flâneur: a Stroll Through the Paradoxes of Paris* (Bloomsbury, 2001)

Christian Wolmar, *The Subterranean Railway* (Atlantic Books, 2012)

Christian Wolmar, *Crossrail: The Whole Story* (Head of Zeus, 2022)

Other books

Anonymous, *Metro de Paris*, Hachette (1969)

David Bownes, Oliver Green and Sam Mullins, *Underground: How the Tube Shaped London* (Penguin, 2012)

Louis Chevalier, *The Assassination of Paris* (University of Chicago Press, 1994)

Arnold Delaney, *Paris by Metro: An Underground History* (Chastleton Travel, 2006)

Samuel Delziani, *Le Petit Inventaire du Metro* (La Vie du Rail, 2016)

David Leboff, *The Underground Stations of Leslie Green* (Capital Transport, 2002)

Andrew Martin, *Underground Overground: A Passenger's History of the Tube* (Profile Books, 2013)

Andrew Martin, *The Winker* (Corsair, 2019)

Julian Pepinster, *Le Metro de Paris* (La Vie du Rail, 2010)

Jean Robert, *Notre Métro* (Jean Robert, 1983)

Gérard Roland, *Paris Métro-Rétro* (Bonneton, 2001)

Grégoire Thonnat, *Petite Histoire du Ticket de Metro Parisien* (Éditions Télémaque, 2019)

Ginette Vincendeau, *Jean-Pierre Melville: An American in Paris* (BFI Publishing, 2003)

Lucy Wadham, *The Secret Life of France* (Faber, 2009)

Filmography

A Run for Your Money, Charles Frend, 1949

Alphaville, Jean-Luc Godard, 1965

Amélie, Jean-Pierre Jeunet, 2001

An American in Paris, Vincente Minnelli, 1951

Bob Le Flambeur, Jean-Pierre Melville, 1956

C'Etait un Rendez-Vous, Claude Lelouch, 1976

Charade, Stanley Donen, 1963

The Clouded Yellow, Ralph Thomas, 1950

The Conformist, Bernardo Bertolucci, 1970

Death Line, Gary Sherman, 1973

Diva, Jean-Jacques Beineix, 1981

Fear Over the City, Henri Verneuil, 1975

French Cancan, Jean Renoir, 1955

Julie and Julia, Nora Ephron, 2009

The Last Metro, François Truffaut, 1980

Last Tango in Paris, Bernardo Bertolucci, 1972

Metroland (TV film), Edward Merzoeff, 1973

Paris Je T'aime, various directors, 2006

The Rebel, Robert Day, 1961

Rififi, Jules Dassin, 1955

Le Samouraï, Jean-Pierre Melville, 1967

Subway, Luc Besson, 1985

Touche Pas à la Femme Blanche, Marco Ferreri, 1974.

The Trial, Orson Welles, 1962.

The Wages of Fear, Georges Clouzot, 1953

Zazie Dans Le Metro, Louis Malle, 1960

Acknowledgements

I would like to thank Nick Alexander, transport map expert; various members of the French Railways Society (http://frenchrailwayssociety.org), especially Michael Bunn; Louisa Dusinberre, for inside information on Parisian life; David Hallgarth, ex of Holdsworth and Co. moquette makers; Brian Hardy, author of *The Paris Metro Handbook* and editor of *Underground News* (the London Underground Railway Society magazine); Sarah Mallinson of Camira Fabrics; Julian Pepinster, Metro expert, author of *Le Metro de Paris* and president of the Association d'Exploitation du Matériel Sprague. Thanks are also due to my 'consultant engineer', whose name I have withheld in case any of his potential clients might object to his opinions, so generously and freely given. I would also (I suppose) like to thank my Francophobe friend, who allowed me to buy him several glasses of good French wine as he slagged off that nation. Finally, I would like to thank my wife, Lisa, for putting up with me as I wrote this book, but she has only herself to blame, really, since she's the one who introduced me to Paris.